What people are saying about …

YES OR NO

"I've long believed the key to success is to make good daily decisions. And it's no easy skill to learn. Any time we spend learning to make better decisions will return a life of blessing. I'm grateful to Jeff Shinabarger for giving us a well-articulated and thoughtful guide. He's just made the future of thousands brighter."

Donald Miller, speaker and bestselling
author of *Blue Like Jazz* and *Storyline*

"It is a joy reading a work written by someone you know, because there is context attached to what they have written. Reading a work about decision making by someone you admire for the decisions they have made in life is an even greater joy. This book was that for me—an inspiring, challenging joy to read. I say yes to this book!"

David Crowder, singer and musician

"Your life's journey is dotted with the decisions you make, which determine your path. In this immensely helpful book, Jeff shows you how to improve your decision-making skills from the inside out. Make the right choice and start reading it today."

Tim Sanders, author of *Love
Is the Killer App: How To Win
Business and Influence Friends*

"Jeff's wisdom has given me great confidence as I have led a major organization. He understands the pressure of making big decisions, the joy and risk that can come from our yes, and the space and wisdom that is born out of the right no. You will be blessed by his words and experience here."

Jennie Allen, author of *Restless*
and founder of IF:Gathering

"In his life, Jeff has repeatedly made courageous decisions. In this course-altering book, he equips you with the tools and framework to make your own courageous decisions. Don't wait to start reading this important book!"

Peter Greer, president and CEO of HOPE
International and coauthor of *Mission Drift*

"Our destiny is the collective result of the day-to-day decisions we make in life. *Yes or No* reminds us of the beauty, wisdom, and life-changing potential that is gifted to us by each moment we experience in life."

Charles Lee, CEO of Ideation and
author of *Good Idea. Now What?*

"Jeff Shinabarger does it again! In his follow-up to *More or Less*, Jeff creates a case for why decision making is so important, especially to leaders. It's part of our job description, and we must make decisions constantly. Jeff provides a road map for decision making that will make you and those around you better equipped for the leadership journey. Take a shot on this book! Say YES!"

Brad Lomenick, author of *The Catalyst Leader*

"*Yes or No* describes the weight we often feel when making decisions for family, work, and life. These two simple words shape everything, and Jeff will help you process any moments of tension and transition."

Rebekah Lyons, author of *Freefall to Fly*

"*Yes or No* offers a brilliant look at the simple decisions of our everyday life. Consequently, Jeff's insights and findings will completely challenge the way you frame your world."

Dale Partridge, founder of Sevenly.org

"Jeff has earned my trust by helping me work through several different nonprofit scenarios. *Yes or No* shows that being a good decision maker isn't just about quickly choosing one option or the other, but about making healthy choices while growing in wisdom and discernment."

Kyle Korver, NBA player, Atlanta Hawks, and founder of Seer Outfitters

YES

— or —

NO

How Your Everyday Decisions
Will Forever Shape Your Life

JEFF SHINABARGER

David C Cook®
transforming lives together

YES OR NO
Published by David C Cook
4050 Lee Vance View
Colorado Springs, CO 80918 U.S.A.

David C Cook Distribution Canada
55 Woodslee Avenue, Paris, Ontario, Canada N3L 3E5

David C Cook U.K., Kingsway Communications
Eastbourne, East Sussex BN23 6NT, England

The graphic circle C logo is a registered trademark of David C Cook.

The website addresses recommended throughout this book are offered as a
resource to you. These websites are not intended in any way to be or imply an
endorsement on the part of David C Cook, nor do we vouch for their content.

LCCN 2014943140
ISBN 978-0-7814-0821-9
eISBN 978-1-4347-0855-7

© 2014 Jeff Shinabarger
Published in association with ChristopherFerebee.com, Attorney and Literary Agent.

The Team: Alex Field, Karen Lee-Thorp, Amy Konyndyk,
Nick Lee, Jack Campbell, Karen Athen
Cover Design: Russell Shaw

Printed in the United States of America
First Edition 2014

1 2 3 4 5 6 7 8 9 10

063014

Love always guides decision makers.
I choose to dedicate this book to
three people I love most:
Andre Jean
Jada Rae
Neko Lee

CONTENTS

ACKNOWLEDGMENTS

This book has only come to life through all of the friendships that have helped me make decisions and the friends who invited me into their decisions. We have navigated difficult life choices together, and I am thankful. To the Plywood Community, this is written to all of you with the hope of greater decisions to come. To every social innovator who has walked through the Plywood Retreat, all of our conversations made this book happen.

Andre, you show me every day how to make choices to show our love to each other and our children, all while pursuing our callings—I could not do it without you. Jada and Neko, I hope you surpass your mom and me, and make impacting decisions for decades to come. Mom and Dad, you have always set a standard for me to accept my role in becoming a person who cares to make things better and walk with others through difficult times. To all my sisters, thank you for walking with me through every turning point in my life, and all the long phone calls to process. To the Ten Hoeve family, thanks for saying Yes to me joining your family and changing my life forever.

Gisele Nelson, you have walked through many times of saying yes and no with me—thanks for living this out every day.

Joanna DeWolf, you have a gift of making things better because you truly love people, and I have always experienced that selfless love from you.

Christopher Ferebee, thanks for the encouragement through the entire process. To the entire team at David C Cook, from editorial to marketing to sales, I know you believe in this and have given it your love—thank you.

To the people sitting at my table and encouraging me to do what they know I am made to do: Jim and Allison Dudley, Greg and Lisa Gilbert, Josh and Katie Thompson, Eric Strickland, Jeremy Blume, Kyle and Juliet Korver, Brad Lomenick, Jimmy Starnes, Sela Missirian, Matt DeWolf, Mike Morin, Robbie and Mimi Brown, Aaron Fortner, Charlie Papparelli, Rick and Lynn Mercer, Steve Franklin, Brett Kirouac, Shane Wheeler, Dan Adamson, Brad Lockwood, Gabe Lyons, Joe Stone, Peyton Day, Leroy Barber, Dan Glaze, John Chambliss, Michael Jones, Daryl Ford, Price Harding, Jack Alexander, Tim Abare, Chris Carneal, Brad Abare, Frank Sabo, Mack Kitchel, Brett Trapp, Matt McKee, Clay Adams, Evan Jones, Josh Guerrieri, Dick Peterson, Reggie Joiner, Joel Iverson, Chet Burge, Joe Danules, Blake Howard, Ben Washer, Ben Farnham, Chelsea Sabo, April Gardner, Anne Seymore, Kerry Wilkerson, Kathryn Taylor, Amanda Vandalen, Anne Curtis, Heather Luyk, George Thomas, Lieze Marie Davis, Scott Helmbold, Russell Shaw, Bobby Callahan, Jared and Eryn Erickson, Erin McClintock, Kay Nwe, Brian Fosse, Alan and Nicole Cheng, and to all the other great friends who have walked through tough choices with me.

✓

CHOOSING
DECISION MAKING

X

1

THIS OR THAT

What Do You Do When You Don't Know What to Do?

In the space between yes and no, there's a lifetime. It's the difference between the path you walk and the one you leave behind; it's the gap between who you thought you could be and who you really are.

Jodi Picoult

I had everything planned out perfectly. Headed to a little sustainable farm in northern Michigan, we were on our way. A four-hour trip loomed ahead of us, and it was just her and me in my Dodge Stratus. A light, fresh snow covered the ground, but nothing that would slow us down. My excitement for what was about to happen made my heart feel like it was three sizes larger than usual and clearly visible through my shirt. Suddenly I realized there was a major element I had not planned on: four hours in the car, just her and me. This day quickly taught me that when a decision is made,

I need to find the clearest and simplest way to communicate it to others.

My girlfriend and I hadn't seen each other for the past week, so the conversation started easily: "What have you been doing this week? I haven't talked to you much; tell me everything." That took all of one mile. Then, "I'm hungry. Let's stop and get some food that we can eat on the way."

We stopped at YaYa's Flame Broiled Chicken, a Shinabarger family favorite with a comfort-food feel. I was in need of some calming comfort. We ordered to go. That bought me thirty minutes. Then I talked about the Michigan State basketball game I had watched the night before, giving more details than usual, anything to fill the empty conversation space.

Next, I turned the tables. "How's your schoolwork going? What's been going on?" At this point, I was pretty sure she could hear the ever-louder thumping of the blood beating through my heart. Turn the radio on to fill that quiet space. Check the directions a few times. Show her a new book I had purchased. Let's listen to this CD. I was thinking of anything we could do without revealing to her what I had really been doing all week.

The stated plan for the evening was night skiing at a ski resort. After reading the book *His Needs, Her Needs*, we were attempting to practice one of the book's suggestions: learning about the things your partner enjoys for recreation and trying to do them with and for each other.[1] I loved to downhill ski, and she was willing to learn. An up-north ski trip provided the perfect excuse to get her in the perfect location for a life-altering question. She thought we were going skiing; sometimes life takes a different direction than our expectations.

About thirty minutes away from our destination, I had run out of conversation starters, so I instructed my beach-loving girlfriend that it was probably time to start dressing for the snow.

"Why don't you add some layers to your outfit? Put on your snow pants, extra layers, gloves, hat …" I was still buying time any way I could. She was all set, and we were pulling into this little farm I wanted to show her before night skiing began. By the time she had bundled up and we rolled out of the car, she looked like the Abominable Snowman, but I didn't care. Outside it was pitch black, and I walked her around in a big circle. I knew this place like the back of my hand and had always wanted to share it with her. We walked through the stables to see all the animals and moved to the back of the property, where the wooden A-frame chapel stood glimmering with soft candlelight shining through the windows. We entered this tiny one-room chapel that seated about twenty people and was set up exactly as I had drawn it out for the groundskeeper. The minute the door opened, she understood what was happening. We slowly walked to the front of the chapel, where I got down on one knee. We were surrounded by beauty, but I could see only one thing in that moment—the eyes of the woman I loved.

She said yes. Her decision changed our lives forever.

DECISIONS CHANGE EVERYTHING

It's amazing how two words have the ability to change everything: *yes* or *no*. Most decisions ultimately come down to the moment when you choose to say yes or choose to say no. I believe that the words *yes* and *no* are the most powerful words in the dictionary. They define what we love, what we will be known for, and what we will do with our lives. These words can both open doors to new places and close doors to old spaces. Yes and no begin new stories and end old plot-lines. They are definitive words: words that significantly change the trajectory of life. When you say yes or no, you give new direction to where you are going and what is still to come. Yes or no determines the hours you will spend in a job. Yes or no makes a commitment to a lifelong relationship. Yes or no shapes your character in times of stress. Yes or no brings you breathlessly to the doctor's office to hear the heartbeat of a child. Yes or no commits you to buy and pay for a car and even a house. Yes or no is what leaves you anxiously waiting to hear if an investor chooses to give your idea funding or supports your social cause to help people in need. Most decisions come down to two small words that define everything. Those two small words are *yes* and *no*.

Choices happen every minute of every day, but some choices have more weight than others. As much as we fret about what to wear in the morning or where to go on the next big date, those moments don't compare with life choices that define where we live, what we do, and who we spend our life with. If you think about the last year, there is a good chance you can remember a minimum of three choices that defined your year. If you consider your entire life, you will recall probably ten to fifteen decisions that defined what you are doing today and the story you are liv-ing. They were defining moments in which you said either yes or no, turning points that forged a path in a different direction toward where you are today. Depending on which little word you use in each situation, it moves you either to a new place or away from that very same place.

Decisions are moments of choice. It's this or that or the other option, and there are often more options than we realize. Decisions start and end with you. I can't make a decision for you; it's on your shoulders. Sometimes that weight on our shoulders is heavy. Oddly enough, the heavier the decisions, the higher our shoulders rise. The tension tightens the neck as the stress seems to yank shoulder muscles up toward our ears.

I like to group decisions into three categories: daily decisions, moments of tension, and transition times.

DAILY DECISIONS

Daily decisions are mundane choices that happen in real time, all the time. It's that moment when a server asks you if you would like a salad with your dinner—yes or no? These are moments of choice that require an instant response but often come from a number of value decisions made earlier. Have I prioritized nutrition, taste buds, or expense? In the book *Blink*, Malcolm Gladwell referred to these daily decisions as "snap judgments … enormously quick; they rely on the thinnest slices of experience. But they are also unconscious." He continues, "We need to respect the fact that it is possible to know without knowing why we know and accept that—sometimes—we're better off that way."[2] Often the cumulative effect of these daily choices or even snap judgments leads you to a destination. For the most part, however, we don't read and buy books looking for answers for the daily decisions. Yet these are the decisions that effectively make us experts on our own daily lives.

From our childhood years, we begin making daily decisions—from what and when we will eat to how and what we will play with others. At times we need to rethink these patterns of daily decisions, but most often they simply become part of what makes each of us unique. We stop needing to learn them or even to think much about them as they naturally flow from who we are.

There are other times of decision, however, that change the trajectory of not only our lives but the lives of others as well. These can be paralyzing moments when we realize we need help. Most of this book will focus on the other two decision periods: moments of tension and transition times. Let's begin unpacking these tension-filled moments when we struggle with understanding what to do.

MOMENTS OF TENSION

I was driving to a lunch meeting at a restaurant in a kind of mall that did not exist twenty years ago: a mall on top of a parking deck. I turned down the ramp to find my spot among the other cars in the concrete jungle. It was midweek and the deck was pretty empty. I intentionally pulled into a parking spot with not a single car around me. I turned the car off and sat motionless. It was one of those shoulder-raising moments. Everyone in my sphere of influence wanted me to make a decision. Nothing felt clear, and everywhere I turned, another problem, choice, or decision called out my name. The numbers on my latest project were lower than expected. My bookkeeper had printed off the latest budget numbers, and they were not looking good. Our next event was looking like it would lose money. My in-box was overflowing with endless emails from my team asking me to make decisions so they could move forward. I felt like I was being a bad father because my stress seemed to sap my ability to give my kids the attention they deserved. Andre (now my wife) was frustrated because I wasn't helping with everything that needed to be done for our family and home. All around me choices yelled out my name, and though they each were yelling loudly, I couldn't seem to focus enough to choose one over another. The options of life became more abundant than my ability to prioritize and choose.

In that moment, all I wanted to do was turn the car back on and drive out of the city. I wanted to leave everything behind. I wanted to quit. Instead I sat in my little Toyota Prius contemplating life. I didn't want to make a decision about how to move forward. I thought, *I could throw my phone out of the window and just drive to a place where not a single person knows my name.* I was done. And at that moment, I never wanted to make another decision again.

However, the other side of me knew I was doing what I was designed to do—I just needed a still moment to make the decisions. I had pushed off too many decisions and wasn't being the leader I was designed to be. I didn't know what to do; there were too many scenarios with too many questions.

So what did I do?

Pulled the keys out of the ignition, opened the door, grabbed my bag, and walked into the restaurant. I took a step forward. Did

I have all the answers? No. But I kept walking. I made the next decision. I moved forward. Lee Iacocca understands: "So what do we do? Anything. Something. So long as we don't just sit there. If we screw it up, start over. Try something else. If we wait until we have satisfied all the answers, it may be too late." We don't have to see the whole staircase, just the first step.

I chose to be a decision maker. I made a choice. I may not have had all the answers, but I had an answer. I decided to move forward and tackle the next question.

Moments of tension often include not just me but a plethora of other people. This is where decision makers emerge: in the midst of problems. As Brad Lomenick, a writer on leadership, has stated, "As long as there are problems in the world, there will be a need for leaders to make the hard choices."[3] If you feel moments of tension and a responsibility to address the problems, there is a good chance you are developing the great responsibility of becoming a decision maker. You are a decision maker if you find yourself in the midst of problem-solving situations continuously and others are looking for you to bring solutions. You choose to solve problems. You see what others don't see and make decisions to change things. You want to make decisions that influence your life, your family's life, and the lives of people around you.

Let me warn you ahead of time: the further you go in decision making, the greater the problems that present themselves to you. But standing in the midst of those tensions is where leaders are needed the most. If you have the potential to be a decision maker, we need you. We need you to push through the tension, tackle one decision at a time, and choose to keep moving.

TRANSITION TIMES

Every so often, the daily decisions and the moments of tension will add up to push you to a transition time. Transition times are often deeply personal when you are wrestling with your calling or career, personal finances, or a life choice like marriage, kids, or buying a house. Transition times have direct implications for what you desire to do, how you choose to live, and major choices of your personal story line. Donald Miller captured this on his blog when preparing for his marriage: "A wedding teaches us that in order to experience meaning we have to make decisions. We can't keep looking at the menu forever, nor can we eat everything on it at once."[4] That's an incredible reminder of how short life really is. Transition times give us both perspective and pain—for example, in that semester when you are about to graduate from college and have to determine what you are actually going to do with your life and where you will live. Or the year you question whether it's time to quit your day job to fully transition to your dream job. Or the month when your credit card bill is more than you can pay and you make lifestyle changes to dig out of a financial deficit. These are transition times—when you change the way you live, when the comfortable place you are in is about to radically turn around.

Both transition times and moments of tension are the points in life when we realize that we desperately need direction, discernment, and ultimately a decision. It's often in these moments when we seek out knowledge, resources, and people to teach us how to decide. We pray and we pray and we pray, hoping for clarity to move forward. They are also the moments when we sometimes have to trust our gut and the wisdom of those most important to us.

YES AND NO

One beautiful November I flew to Los Angeles to spend a full day dreaming and planning a book with my great friend Charles Lee. We are both idea people with great admiration for one another, and we were going to write a collaborative book about idea making. (He has since written his own book on the topic that is excellent.) We outlined 80 percent of the book, and I thought it was good. Our individual homework assignments were to begin our first couple of chapters to further explore the tensions of writing together while working out our collective writing voice.

En route home that night, my adrenaline was flying just as high as the airplane. I couldn't wait to tell Andre all about it. I vividly remember sitting down with her the next day and telling her all our ideas, fully expecting her to be as excited as I was. She quickly brought me down to earth. She had this sense that I shouldn't do it. She said no. It wasn't because she didn't want me to work with Charles; she loves him. It wasn't that she didn't think the concept was good; she thought it was a great topic for both of us to share and explore. She just didn't feel good about it. My heart sank as I called Charles to apologize and tell him I could not participate. There was really no reason, but we both knew the choice needed to be made. I chose that day to trust my wife, who we realized in hindsight had a hunch about something on the horizon that I didn't see. It's important to listen to the people we love; they often see or sense things we don't.

Sometimes we make choices and sometimes others' choices determine what life looks like for us. Not every decision is made solely by ourselves or for ourselves. As we accept that we live in a world where we are not islands but rather interconnected webs of people, we must learn to give and take with others as we make decisions. Sometimes when decisions are made for us, the only thing we can do is choose to respond to the new challenges. How we respond to others' choices will reveal what we value and who we desire to become.

Just two months after that moment of decision, on a routine Thursday afternoon, I was in a meeting with two friends planning an event. My phone rang twice in a row from my wife. This was our previously agreed-upon sign that it was an emergency for which I needed to stop everything I was doing to answer. I walked into the other room as Andre burst out the words, "We have been matched." Lost in event-planning mode, I did not quite pick up her train of thought. I asked, "To what?"

"We have been matched with a baby."

"A baby?" I replied incredulously.

"Yeah. I just got the call. It's a little girl. She was born ten days ago, here in Atlanta, and they are asking if we want to adopt her. We would pick her up on Monday."

I am fully convinced that my eyebrows immediately lifted higher than my hairline. My mind started racing. *Monday? Baby? I'm going to be a dad?*

Andre waited for a moment before asking, "So can I tell them yes?"

"*Yes!* Yes, of course!"

Her name is Jada.

We called our family and close friends. Then we did what all good young Americans would do in that moment: We updated our Facebook status to tell the world that we were becoming parents—on

Monday. And that we had nothing, no car seat, no diapers, no paci-
fier, no bottles; we had absolutely nothing for a child.

Over the course of three days, every corner of our community
overwhelmed us with gifts. Their generosity was humbling. They
gave us crash courses in bottles and diapers and even threw us the
fastest-ever-planned baby shower. Through the entire adoption
process, the greatest gift was not from our community; it was
from a mother who had carried our Jada for eight months while
she was homeless on the streets of Atlanta. While taking care of
two other children who had great needs, she freely gave my wife
and me her baby with nothing in return. She said yes to us. We
said yes to her. Our community said yes to two that became three
in a few short days. At some point around that whirlwind time,
another wave of gratefulness came over me as I remembered how
my wife had somehow known it was the wrong time to say yes
to a book project. And I had trusted Andre's intuition enough to
listen and choose.

CHOOSE YOUR ADVENTURE

Day after day, you choose your future. Sometimes other people make
decisions that affect you, but you still choose your response as a part
of the equation of what happens next. Many decisions are easy, but
some weigh more than others. I am thankful that we were created in
a way to make decisions; we were given the choice of how to live and
what to believe. I do believe that in the end God will have ultimate
determination of the world, but we have been granted the freedom
to live and make choices in this beautiful and broken world. Even

in environments controlled by others, we always have the option to follow that law or direction, or not.

Choices are constant. What our lives look like will be determined by a series of decisions we make continuously. Life is a lot like a Choose Your Own Adventure book. Our lives can be great adventures. As in the book, we can go back and review the choices we have made and realize what may have brought us to where we are. The difference between our lives and a page-turning book is that we can't go back and start over. The decisions we make are made. Therefore, it is in the page-turning times that we often need some guidance.

Our choices determine our future. Inevitably, a transition (and tension) time is in your new future. It's simply a matter of when. Consider this list of some of the life-shaping decisions we all make in our lives, sometimes more than once:

> **Education:** What school should I enroll in? What about my child(ren)? What should be the focus of my studies? How high of a degree should I complete?
> **Career:** What job should I take? What am I made to do? When should I quit my day job to fulfill my dream job? I feel like my purpose is being unfulfilled; what should I do next? How do I balance career and kids? What problems do I want to solve with my life?
> **Relationships:** Should I get married? How do I find a partner? Should I have children? When and how many? Do we feel a calling toward adoption?

Home: Where should I live and why? Should I go larger or downsize? Should I rent or buy? How are we going to renovate this place?

Money: What is enough? Where should I give? How do I get out of debt? How should I invest for the future? How do I make more? When should I retire? How are we going to pay this month's bills?

Community: Should I tell friends my opinion on their situations? I want to give my time and talents to something significant, but where should I serve? What am I most passionate about for my community, and what can I uniquely give? Who do I spend my time with, and what do we do together?

Team: Who do I want to work for and with? Can we afford another person on the team? Which person should I hire? Which person am I going to let go from the job, and how am I going to tell that person? Should we dream bigger or tighten up our budget? How am I going to pay the bills at the end of the month? Can I get the funding?[5]

The questions keep coming in every stage of life. Whether it's far in the future or right in front of you, it's always a good time to consider your process for making a crucial decision. Sadly, I can't tell you what to decide. (Imagine how successful I would be if I could!) I do, however, believe I can assist you in becoming a decision maker.

The key question I am asking throughout this book is simply: What do you do when you don't know what to do? My hope is to offer you some practical ways to navigate when the path to yes or no is difficult to discern. I want to give you action points to assist you in thinking through how you make choices not just on your own but alongside the people you love and trust. May the ideas in this book provide you with a framework for making decisions about life's relentless choices, some more significant than others, but all creating the life you get to live each day.

TAKE ACTION

At the end of every chapter, I will provide an action step to make the ideas concrete. What moment of tension or transition do you find yourself processing today?

What many of us do when we don't know what to do is avoid the tough decision. Stop for a moment and consider whether you have been avoiding a decision in your life. It could be related to work or family or any other arena in your life. Take some time to write out the dilemma as you currently see it. Pinpoint the problem so that you can accurately address the issue at hand. Stick that paper right in this book so you can refer back to it. Let us commit to working through this problem together as you continue reading this book.

QUESTIONS FOR GROUPS

1. What three choices defined the past year for you? These could be choices that changed things or that kept things the same as they were.

2. What are some of the decisions that have defined what you are doing today and the story you are living?

3. What challenges do you face with regard to making decisions? For instance, do you tend to avoid decisions? Do you decide quickly and later regret it? Do you tend to see too many options? Too few?

2

MY STORY

What Is Your Coconut Calling?

I won't tell you that the world matters nothing, or the world's voice,
or the voice of society. They matter a good deal. They matter far
too much. But there are moments when one has to choose between
living one's own life, fully, entirely, completely—or dragging
out some false, shallow, degrading existence that the world in
its hypocrisy demands. You have that moment now. Choose!

Oscar Wilde

Change goes hand in hand with decisions. If you don't like change, you will have a difficult time making decisions. Change is made more difficult if we don't have a sense of what we're made to do and where we're going. Stephen R. Covey said, "The key to the ability to change is a changeless sense of who you are, what you are about and what you value."[1] Decisions rely on a keen sense of who we are and what we are about. Without this clarity of life purpose, we will continually struggle to make life decisions. Without clarity about what we are trying to become, we won't be able to process decisions that take us down the paths headed in the right direction.

The most terrifying moments of transition come when we are dissatisfied with our current reality yet lack clarity regarding our future direction. We have all experienced these moments of desperation when we feel stuck and in need of direction. Deep down we long for our lives to have meaning, and we want that meaning to give purpose to our daily lives, but we have not made that connection. As a result, everyday life is frustrating. We sense there is something more but have not figured out what that might be. This is why self-help books sell millions every January; they promise a different you, a better you with greater satisfaction and self-worth. It is why the average twentysomething stays in a job for only eleven months. It is the age-old question: Why am I here and what am I going to do with my life?

Let me assure you that answering these questions is a lifelong pursuit. Very few people figure out their unique calling at age sixteen and consistently follow that path the rest of their lives. Instead, I have noticed in my own life and in the lives of those I have walked alongside over the years that these questions are often explored in stages throughout our lives.

At each stage, life is meant to be lived. Wherever you are in your journey, fully embrace the experiences you live in right now, because these experiences prepare for tomorrow. Some people let the uncertainty paralyze them, keeping them from trying new things and making discoveries as they live.

None of your past experiences are wasted. In fact, quite the contrary, every experience helps you move closer to where you want to be and who you are intended to become. Even if you discover that this is not the way you want to live for the rest of your life, you have come closer to who you are meant to be.

CARVING THE COCONUT

During one of the biggest transition stages in my life, my wife, daughter, and I lived in Nicaragua for three months. At least twice a week we rented bikes from my friend Baker, founder of Bicimaximo. He had started a social enterprise in Granada that was employing men coming out of addiction recovery programs, jail, or both. These guys were proactively choosing a new story for their lives by working hard every day to serve tourists wanting an adventure bike ride.

We were the first people at the bike shop to request a bike seat for a child. Our daughter, Jada, was nearly two years old and part of our adventure, so we needed a way to include her in our bicycle excursions. They quickly unburied a single child seat from storage that someone had given them. Baker was excited to try out this new seat, so he had his team weld the seat to a bike for us to use. We tied her in with a rope. (Not all countries are quite as "child safety device" oriented as the United States. Go figure.)

We rented bikes (the bike with the child seat was always available) and followed a road for about five miles that dead-ended at a dock and restaurant on Lake Nicaragua. It was one of the most life-giving things we did while we were away. It gave us time to exercise, think, and process life while riding through the streets and culture of Granada. I resonate with what Ernest Hemingway once said, "It is by riding a bicycle that you learn the contours of a country best, since you have to sweat up the hills and coast down them." Seeing the country while on two wheels made us love Nicaragua.

Every ride, we passed the Coconut Guy on the way to the dock. To this day I couldn't tell you his name, yet he and his coconut stand profoundly shaped the way I think about calling. He gave me a metaphor for my progress in calling.

He had a four-foot-square plywood board propped up on top of a five-gallon paint bucket, balanced just perfectly so as not to fall off one side or the other. Taped to the front of the bucket was a piece of paper with a sharpie message that simply communicated "$1" with an arrow pointing up. The marketer in me loves simple signs that require just enough imagination to get your attention. Following the direction of the arrow up, you quickly realized that he was sitting under a coconut tree. The process was simple. You handed him a dollar and he shimmied up the tree, picked a green coconut fresh from the tree, and brought it back down. He would then set the coconut on his perfectly balanced plywood and bucket table and with a machete start quickly and methodically carving the sides of the green coconut until the white heart of the fruit appeared. It took him just a minute to shape it into a cuplike design, puncture the top, stick a straw inside, and hand it over to the paying customer. Voilà! A fresh coconut drink made right in front of your eyes.

Every time I saw this process, it made me think about what I am designed to be and do. As I watched the Coconut Guy carve off the edges with each whack of the machete, I thought of all the different things I had tried in my life. Things that seemed like a good fit for me but didn't quite match my abilities and loves. Whack. I like doing this but fail miserably when I try to do that. Whack. This is something I love to do but never can find the time to do. Whack. Each life experience, each decision I make, each time I succeed or fail sheds off another dirty, crusty edge and moves closer to the best part. Just another step in the process of finding the tasty, milky core. Those bike rides gave me a lot of time to think about my life and the things I had shed on the way to discovering my life purpose. Without shaving things off our life, we will never find our ultimate purpose. These decisions that define purpose separate decision makers from everyone else.

FINDING MY PURPOSE

I started at a very young age working on a national event called Catalyst. Catalyst is a leadership event for next generation leaders. I became the creative leader of this community when I was just twenty-four years old. Every day I was wrestling through the tensions of being a young leader in my own life, which positioned me well to direct the brand. While we saw a lot of success, I failed hard, fast, and often.

When I started, we had just one event that gathered about five thousand people annually. In the first event I led, we had the most confusing speaker to ever grace our stage. He is a best-selling author, an incredible writer and dreamer, but as a speaker he did not connect with our audience at all. He was scheduled to speak on both days. After the first day, I had to make the call. What was I going to do? Was I going to simply let it ride and allow him to share a second time or confront the issue and ask him not to speak the second day? It quickly occurred to me that my choice involved balancing the importance of creating the best experience for five thousand people or choosing to care about the feelings of one person. At times, decision making means you make the good choice for the most people while disappointing a few. Making tough choices is not fun, but it will always make you a better leader. My partner and I asked him not to speak a second day. It was a difficult situation, but I exponentially grew as a decision maker by choosing a decision I didn't want to make.

Over the years, a few of us collectively grew the brand to have large-scale success reaching twenty-five thousand people annually through in-person events around the country. We created what Michael Hyatt, author of a world-renowned leadership blog, called a platform, "something you stand on to be seen and heard.... Today, a platform is about leading a tribe of engaged followers."[2] In the midst of teaching about leadership, our team had the opportunity to introduce leaders around the nation to issues of injustice and people giving their lives to fight against that injustice.

Over time I transitioned from holding a full-time job at Catalyst to being a freelance consultant working on the event elements that most interested me. Strangely, though, I began to sense that this was not all there was for me. I had an annual contract for a sizable amount of money with the freedom to work as much or as little as I wanted. Budget was never a problem, and dreaming big was encouraged. I believed in the vision and felt like I consistently helped guide a large community to new places. In a freelance economy, this was the consultant's dream work. Deep down, though, I knew that everything I was designed to be and do was not being fulfilled.

It's common that passionate and talented decision makers lead organizations, but behind known brands there are still real people with personal purposes and tensions that don't always fully match the mission of the work. Just because we are doing something that looks incredible on the outside doesn't mean we are living everything we are intended to live. We may find success for a season on a project, but that doesn't always mean we should give our lives to that cause.

While I was wrestling with this tension, I had an insightful life-planning process with a coach, Pete Richardson. He bluntly gave me his opinion: "If this is all that God had designed for you … you would probably be dead. There is a good chance this is preparing you for something more. God is not done with you yet." Once I got over the morbid part of the advice, it felt liberating. Gut-wrenchingly honest thoughts like these are equally motivating and terrifying. He was right. Deep down I always had this feeling of tension, of not fully living what I was designed to be, and knew there would be a moment when I would need to transition.

Yet another life-shaping opportunity came when I was invited to partner with a great visionary named Gabe Lyons. Gabe has an enormous vision to change the widely held negative perceptions of American Christianity, and he has many long-term strategies to make this vision come to life. Our society has come to see Christians according to what they are against and no longer what they are for. He has a gift of seeing culture and translating faith in a way that connects with culture instead of retreating from it. He is the type of guy who values innovation but wrestles with what those innovations will mean to the character and soul of a person.

While we were together, we launched an event called Q. Q convenes proven cultural leaders for conversation, reflection, and action that renew culture.[3] Through this community, I had the opportunity to meet some of the most influential people in all aspects of society. To say it was a privilege would be an understatement. We hosted gatherings that brought together leaders from seven different channels of culture: government, arts and entertainment, business, the social sector, media, education, and the church. After a few years of his work, Gabe made a strategic decision to move the headquarters from Atlanta to New York City, the cultural epicenter of the world. He invited me to join him in the move.

Andre and I boarded a plane to New York City to consider what life might look like if we lived in this new place. Two friends went with us, and we had a blast. We traveled all over the city and barely slept. We tasted the food, walked and rode on the streets and subway, experienced the entertainment, and connected with friends. We loved it. The moment I'll never forget, though, was sitting on the runway waiting to head back to Atlanta. Leaning over to Andre, I asked the million-dollar question, "What do you think?" She smiled and with the utmost clarity said, "I had an amazing time. I don't think we are supposed to move to New York."

I sat back with a smile on my face because my feelings were exactly the same. It was clear; we were feeling more and more called to live in and shape the future of Atlanta. It was the end of a time of our life and a transition toward a refined calling. That vision was my friend's vision, and it was time to shave that off to move closer to my purpose. John C. Maxwell taught me at an early age, "Learn to say no to the good so you can say yes to the best."[4]

SAYING NO TO SAY YES

Every time I say no to something in moments of transition, elements of my unique design become clearer. The people I've interacted with, the specific job duties I've put into action, and the ideas I've wrestled with in each of my jobs and life experiences have contributed to a clear picture of who I am and what I love.

First, I love to work and dream with people giving their lives to solving problems. People who don't take the easy road. They choose the road less traveled, and it makes a difference. More often than not, they choose a calling that improves life for other people. They value this more than making money for themselves. These people have innovative approaches to addressing social issues that plague the places where we live. I love to help them expand, sustain their efforts, dream at new levels, and share their stories with others. I've learned that I'm good at it and want to do it more. I enjoy doing the hard work with them and seeing them succeed.

The second thing I've learned is that I am a uniquely creative individual. I have the ability to think of creative concepts more than the average person. Others call me creative, and I need to use that ability more. I need to have the freedom to create and the space in my work life to create. My creativity can breathe life into a new leader's dreams and ideas. I have something to offer to others.

The third thing I've learned is that I have a unique role in society and I must use it wisely. Dr. Martin Luther King Jr. used to walk out his front door and instantly be confronted with some of the most marginalized people of the city. But on that same day, he also had the opportunity to sit at a table with the most influential leaders of the city. I believe he was very intentional about staying close to both groups. I feel like I have been presented with a similar opportunity. I grew up attending an inner-city high school and have now chosen to live in the heart of Atlanta. I've known rich and poor and everything in between, and I'm comfortable being with just about everyone. I believe I have a unique role to play in bridging gaps between the poor and the rich and in creating dialogues between these people groups that don't know each other but would be better off if they did. These two groups need each other, and I have a unique ability to bring them together, to bridge communities and create new solutions to social problems. I truly believe that both communities have the potential to benefit significantly through relationship with each other.

Those three realizations and all the experiences I had up to that point eventually led to my decision to start my own nonprofit organization, a social enterprise called Plywood People. I found a way to put together my unique skills, abilities, and connections to serve a group of people I love. Our goal is to build a community of social innovators in the city of Atlanta. I began hiring a team and quickly saw potential. Those first years were thrilling and terrifying all at once. I started to pursue those things I loved and felt skilled to do.

We ramped up Gift Card Giver publicity, started the billboard bag project employing and training refugees, and began networking and consulting with social innovators. We launched Plywood Presents, an event to inspire, connect, and educate social innovators in Atlanta. I started leading Plywood Retreats to provide intentional coaching for social start-ups. The foundation was set and my vision was becoming clearer. It was a liberating and energizing part of my journey.

MORE CARVING

The ideas and the work came fast and furious, but I still had only twenty-four hours in every day. My start-up had a unique funding plan. I did outside paid consulting with about a third of my time in order to pay for the financial needs of my family, while leading as a full-time volunteer of Plywood People.

About three years in, I could sense that it was time for a change. It was time to move past balancing my day job with my dream calling. In order for the organization to move into the next phase of predicable success, it needed a full-time leader. There was an opportunity gap, and I needed to fill the space with focused time and energy. Every moment I was not focused on developing work I was limiting the progress of the organization.

I was sitting in another moment of transition. I was doing two jobs, and neither was getting the full attention necessary. I needed to choose a direction with the next phase of my calling, to say yes to what I was made to do and say no to the things that I could do but others ought to do. I needed to shave off the elements of the coconut that were distracting me from the core of my design, what my friend Ken Coleman would call "the sweet spot."

These questions swirled through my head when Bob Goff gave me his trademark advice to "quit something." Andre and I both sensed that we were at a transition point and needed time to sort things out. So we did more than just quit something; we quit most everything. Andre took a sabbatical from work, I finished all my urgent contract work, and we took our daughter to live in Nicaragua for three months. I wrote my first book, and Andre and I worked through the process of solidifying who we were and what we wanted to be about as a family.

TAKE THE TIME

When I returned, I can honestly say that I had the clearest sense of purpose I have ever had in my life. Why is that? I took the time and I worked a process. I took a moment to stand back and evaluate what I was made to do with my life and why I was doing it. When you step away from the hustle that makes up daily living and reevaluate that hectic pace, it is common to begin to see things more clearly. I would never have had that clarity unless I had chosen to say no to everything for a period and process my God-given abilities, on-the-ground skills, and unique experiences to that point.

Times of transition often naturally give us the opportunity of time, but filled with the fear of the unknown, we quickly move toward any solution in order to fill time, meet the budget, and move on. Why is it that as a culture, the minute we lose a job or are in a transition, the question we ask each other is, what are you going to do next? This is an unhealthy pressure to put on one another. I wish we encouraged our friends to take times of transition to slow their pacing and find clarity before they move on to another workplace.

Transition times give us the opportunity to step back and ponder our purpose. If we don't take advantage of these moments, we will too often continue to move forward feeling dissatisfied with work and relationships and ultimately life itself. The flip side is to take a time of rest and consider the aspirations that match our love, story, and dreams.

Eddie Kirkland[5] is a gifted musician who asked me to talk through some major transitions he was walking through. For years he had been leading worship for North Point Community Church (an incredible role of influence), but he sensed a transition coming. He was feeling something new emerging and was asking my advice about how to transition his role. I recommended not trying to figure it out while he was still consumed in his current role. I knew his family could take a few months off to ponder what was next.

At first, this concept seemed impossible and almost irresponsible for a father and husband. But his family chose to do it. They took an extended time of rest, reflection, and prayer to consider what was next. I remember having dinner with him and his wife—they revealed the vision they had of starting the Parish, a new collective of Anglican churches in the Atlanta area.[6] It was a perfect mix of what he loved, what his story had prepared him for, and what problem he felt called to solve. Eddie is a great example of what can happen if we take the time to understand what we are uniquely designed to do. Not only did he find clarity, he found energy to pursue this new vision together with his wife, Danielle.

The more we understand what we should not do, the more a resonant picture emerges of what we ought to do. We must focus our attention to let go of what we can do to pursue a problem we are made to solve.

We all know in theory that deep down within each of us is something unique, something special. But it takes working through the outer elements to get to the core of what we are designed to do and be. I witnessed this same idea of carving off the edges on a trip to Italy in college. Our trip included a visit to the Galleria dell'Accademia in Florence where Michelangelo's *David* resides. For three hours, I sat with a journal and pen next to the seventeen-foot spectacular creation, overwhelmed with its beauty. Out of a single block of marble and four years of work, this depiction of the famous Bible character took a shape unmatched in history. From one block of matter came a story of beauty. When you choose to live what you are designed to be, it inspires others to find that same purpose in life. But craftsmanship or curating your calling will take time.

This book is an invitation to step back, take time, and process as you consider your next decision. Of course, making time necessitates saying no to something. Too often we try to adorn our lives with other things that make us look the way the culture accepts, but to shine uniquely we need to carve down toward our inner and most purposeful designs. The process of learning what to say no to only gets us closer to what we ought to say yes to. We can't be bashful in understanding what to get rid of; knowing what we should not do is very valuable in getting to what we will do.

When I stop and think about all the busyness that fills my life, I often know there are things I should stop doing, but rarely do I cut them out of my life. The only way to find your unique calling is by saying no to those things that are not your calling. Say no to expectations that others have of you. Say no to choices that are good in order to find options that are better. Say no to opportunities that will lead you away from problems you feel called to address and some day will become known for solving.

Dr. Henry Cloud and Dr. John Townsend call this creating boundaries: "[Boundaries] define *what is me* and *what is not me*. A boundary shows me where I end and someone else begins, leading me to a sense of ownership."[7] Clearly defining our boundaries and our abilities more quickly helps us accomplish all that we desire: "Say no to the unimportant, and say no to the inclination to do less than your best. If you are doing your best work on the most important things, you will reach your goals."[8]

If *yes* and *no* are the two most powerful words in the dictionary, we need to take ownership of how and when to use them as an intentional practice. Saying no will increase the opportunities for where you ought to say yes.

MOVING FORWARD

To progress in this next phase of my calling was going to demand a deep courage to overcome the fear of the unknown future. I had many fears about finances and security and ultimately failure. But once I had taken the time to sort through who I was and where I wanted to be, I discovered the foundation I needed to move forward. I started realizing the work I was doing was directly related to the things I love to do and the people I love to serve. I had the knowledge through experience and education, and others were affirming it. My vision was clear: I want to be known as a problem solver. An influencer helping create solutions, then helping to sustain those new solutions to some of the world's biggest problems while being rooted in local community.

This was where I also confronted the deep-seated issue of personal motivation. To leap into the leadership of a start-up nonprofit organization rooted in a greater community in a way that it could support my family was going to mean that I would be reliant on others. Until this point, I had been primarily self-reliant, especially in the financial arena. My biggest fears centered on finances. Money has never been a driver for me in life, but when others are dependent on me, money is essential. Not only did I need to provide for my family, I also now felt responsible for my team and their families. The fact of the matter is that 100 percent security is not possible if we are pursuing problem solving in a new way. This put me in a precarious position. Was I willing to lose my self-reliance and ambition and open myself up to ask others to help me? Did I believe that God would provide for me? Frankly, it felt easier to assert my own control of the future. But I started realizing that this dream was bigger than me. I was just the human chosen to make it come to life.

I finally decided to give it my all. Yes. My spirit resonated with the eloquent words of Georgia O'Keeffe: "Whether you succeed or fail is not important. Making the unknown known is what is important." I was ready to pursue the next phase of my calling. It passed through my philosophy-of-choice process—I had good motives, the things and people I loved were in support of it and would be served by the calling, the choice lined up with my past story, and I had been given a vision of where my calling and dreams lined up. I was willing to move forward with good intentions, knowing I could fail, knowing others would push back, knowing not everyone would understand, and knowing it would take more than my single abilities.

Even after this clarity, it took me another nine months before I transitioned completely into a full-time employee of Plywood People. During that time, I walked through a process of turning the ideals into tangibles and working out how to make this happen with the people willing to do it all with me. All throughout this time I was praying for wisdom and praying that I would be surprised by the confirmation of others.

The first task was to clearly determine the options for how to proceed and the timeline of the transition. There were three legitimate options: end consulting and become the executive director of Plywood People as a full-time employee, find a different leader to be the full-time executive director for Plywood People and become an adviser, or shut down Plywood People altogether and move in a new direction. The last option at times seems extreme, but I always think having the option of exiting an idea is important to make sure our passion is still fully engaged in our work. Exiting ought to always be on the table. We are taught at an early age that quitting is a bad choice, and at times it is; but as we get older, we need to foster the practice of communicating no, and that means we will need to learn the art of quitting. But I was still passionate about this work, so quitting was not the best option. I knew deep down that the most courageous option would be to pursue this dream with my whole mind and heart, but it was the most fear-filled direction. I needed to take the next step forward.

Next was considering who would be influenced by this decision. First up was Andre; she wanted me to stop consulting before I even started. She was all in and had fewer fears than I did. My team and board of directors were all eager to have me fully engaged and believed there would be a positive outcome.

Second, I went to seek counsel from the people who believe in me and know my best abilities and worst habits to gain an outward perspective. They helped me think through all the options and a timeline of how to move forward. They knew this was the right direction and affirmed my calling.

Now I had to come to grips with my own fears. I left the city for a day to think, dream, and pray. In every major transition I need to ponder my request before God for spiritual contentment. On days like these, I will always have fears, but I also need a sense of peace and direction. I was overwhelmed with the burden of doing something I had never done before and equally felt a clear calling from God that I would be taken care of in every scenario. That day I walked and walked and walked, trying to think of every way not to do this work, but knowing confidently it was the right direction.

Lastly, I had to share with the clients I was contracted to serve. They understood but asked for a little transition time to help find replacements for my work. In every way possible, leave past partners in a good next place.

It was time to move beyond the security of my past to pursue problems that I have been called to solve. Three questions guided my philosophy of choice: What do you love? What wisdom have you uniquely been given? And what problem have you been called to solve? As we move into the next three chapters, we are going to dig into your philosophy of choice to process those questions for your story.

TAKE ACTION

I share my story to help you see the very personal context that sets up the rest of the book. More than simply hypothesizing or reading and reporting on research, I have lived the transitions, the choices, and the processes. If you are in a time of transition, my challenge to you at this point is twofold:

> 1. Where do you need to say no to create opportunities to say yes?
>
> 2. How will you set aside time to work on this process? While I highly recommend an extended amount of time, even a week or a weekend, if you are in a major time of transition, there are other ways to accomplish it. Could you mark on your schedule a block of hours every week to process through the book and your thinking? Take the time.

QUESTIONS FOR GROUPS

1. How is finding your life purpose like carving a coconut? Have you experienced this carving? If so, how?

2. What are some of the things you have said no to in the past? How have these decisions brought you closer to your purpose? Have any of these decisions taken you further from your purpose, or have they just taken you sideways? If so, which ones? What has saying no taught you?

3. How do you respond to the idea of stepping away from activities for a time in order to make decisions about a transition? What are the risks and costs of doing this? What are the benefits?

✓

YOUR PHILOSOPHY
OF CHOICE

X

3

I HEART

What Do You Love?

*Do not hesitate to love and love deeply. You might be afraid
of the pain that love can cause.... As you love deeply, the
ground of your heart will be broken more and more, but you
will rejoice in the abundance of the fruit it will bear.*

Henri Nouwen

Brad is the kind of guy who loves people well. He came to a Plywood
Retreat while he was smack-dab in the middle of a transition time.
It's typical that on the second day of our retreat, people start getting
overwhelmed with the amount of information they are processing,
so we force them to hand in their phones and take two hours for
solitude. Half of them excitedly turn over their devices while the
other half grudgingly pry their fingers away from the precious glass
screens. We send them all over the farm with a set of processing

questions. Everyone is given the freedom to explore alone, and we try to stay out of the way.

This time, though, Brad and I crossed paths. We leaned against a flower-covered walkway to talk. I could tell Brad was processing something big. We had a lengthy conversation about how he knew there was something else he ought to be doing but didn't know what. Already, Brad actively sought to make a difference in his world. Over the years he had run national campaigns to collect socks for the homeless, united musicians for benefit concerts and albums, and mobilized students to serve and use their gifts toward action. He was young and had already accomplished much. But he could sense more was yet to come.

He has a brother-in-law named Robby. Robby has a way of walking into any room and owning it as if he were the president, at the age of eight. Just a few months after the retreat, presidential candidates campaigned across the United States seeking office. Robby and Brad decided to make a little video that showed Robby joining the election trail as Kid President, where he encouraged others with the upbeat message "Don't be in a party. Be a party."[1] It started gaining momentum, and by the fourth video, it went viral as the YouTube sensation Pep Talk.

As millions of people connected to the messages of Kid President, opportunities started flooding Brad and Robby. Swiftly Brad's sense of something-to-come morphed into the thick of decision making. Nothing had prepared them for the number of ideas, expectations, and opportunities lining up at their door. They became overwhelmed by the external pressure and crazy demands forced upon their family.

The family decided to stop everything and determine what they loved and what they wanted to create. Brad said, "There are many people who have a direction for us, a plan for us. But I don't think that is where we want to go. We have to stay on our path. Put our stake in the ground. This is the path we are going to go on, and we are going to stay true to that." Though money tempted and fame enticed, they determined to stay with what they really love. They love to encourage and challenge kids to do great things, and they do it really, really well. They found their love.

What you love and whom you love should always be the starting place for decision making. Your loves should shape your choices. But how do you know what it is you really love?

SIGNS OF LOVE

We make decisions that match our love. If I were to ask you right now, "What do you love?" you may quickly offer me the "right" answer, but it may not honestly match the love deep inside you. Most of us have many different loves, but as decision makers we must prioritize our loves.

A few years ago, a golf game with Jim and Garrick radically affected my view of love. I knew Jim really well but was still getting to know Garrick. We were on the second hole and I asked him, "What do you really love?" He was temporarily stunned by the question. He mentioned his family and his faith, both authentic and true answers. But then he shoved his golf club in his bag and looked warily at me, as if I were not ready for what he was about to say. "What I really love? I love cooking crawfish!"

He was right; I was not ready for that answer. He is the only person I have ever heard say something like this. For you non-southerners, crawfish are bottom feeders with pinchers like a crab but the body size of a shrimp. It is a great southern tradition to invite a crowd of friends over to boil and eat crawfish together. Three straight holes of golf later, I was still listening to the details of Garrick's crawfish-boiling love. From the live crawling creatures picked up at the market to the apron and hat he wears throughout the boiling day, he loves every single minute of the process. He loves teaching people how to eat crawfish, from the perfect blend of seasoning right down to how to suck the juice from the head. He even loves the cleanup. From start to finish, his best days of the year include boiling crawfish.

Since then, Garrick and I have collaborated to provide an outlet for his love in a way that helps our nonprofit organization raise money: the Annual Crawfish and Cornhole Tournament. When you experience the love that Garrick has for this craft, something in you stirs. It reminds you of what you love and who you are when that love is alive in you. Love is contagious.

Sometimes that contagious love even unearths a love buried long ago. We bury our loves for all sorts of reasons: peer pressure, fear of ridicule, past wounds. You may have already judged my friend Garrick and his unique crawfish-boiling love, but that's actually the point: uniqueness. When you experience Garrick's unique love, you realize that all of us are unique. We were created to live out that unique love. It is meant to be shared. And when we share love, love spreads.

It took me just a few minutes in my friend Brett's home to find his love. The house was stacked with a hodgepodge of historical artifacts he had found from antique shops and sales across the region. From an American flag with thirteen stars, to a stained-glass image of Jesus, to a new creation he and a friend designed and called a Typelighter. A Typelighter is an antique typewriter reconstructed into a lamp, using the space bar to turn the lamp on and off. He loves to find one-of-a-kind items from back in the day and reclaim them through story.

When I pinpointed this in conversation, his face lit up. Immediately he began to share his childhood dream to be an archaeologist. It started as a simple conversation and ended with a friend sharing a major part of his life with me. His love drives his free time; he spends hours picking through junk in out-of-the-way places to find the hidden gems. Like his collection of Typelighters, every item in his space has a story of where he found it and what makes it significant.

When we identify and prioritize what we love, it brings us life and revives us. The moment Brett and Garrick started sharing their loves, the life within them was infectious and caused everyone else around them to want to learn more. I don't love antiques or crawfish, but I love that they love those things. It makes me want to encourage them to share their loves with more people.

SHOW ME THE MONEY

Something about the people and things we love takes hold of us in inexplicable but real ways. It starts to steal our time away and we don't even mind. We look for ways to simply be with the things we love—or better yet, the people we love—even when it means shortchanging other areas of our lives. Where we spend our time and money reveals our loves. We instinctively prioritize love through decision making.

When given a choice, where do you spend your time or money and with whom? My preacher dad used to say, "Do you want me to tell you what is important to you? Give me your calendar and your checkbook." One of the most vulnerable things an American can do is reveal their spending habits.

Greg is a financial adviser who has served as a leader on our organizational board. He repeatedly offered to help my family with our personal finances. I tried to push it off, but he kept encouraging us to meet. I found this to be one of the most nerve-racking first-time meetings I have experienced (and I have had a lot of first-time meetings). Spreading out all my personal financial information felt like putting all my dirty laundry on a table and hearing what someone else had to say about it. I knew he would ask questions about every debt, investment, and purchase. He would probably ask about my dreams, which sometimes feel foolish, unattainable, unable to survive scrutiny from an outsider.

Once I got over my initial anxiety and sat down with Greg, it was like a weight fell off my shoulders. Rather than judgment, Greg gave me an outside perspective of wisdom. He looked at the ways we spent our money and gave me his observations of what I loved. I needed to hear what someone else saw as my loves. Contrary to the age-old saying, we all put our money not where our mouths are but where our hearts are day after day.

Money plays a significant role in decision making not just in our personal lives but also in our professions. Many people change jobs for the opportunity to make more money. If you are moving to a new job, the unwritten but clearly understood expectation includes a pay raise. The challenge of this common practice is that money is rarely a match for finding that core that is tied closely to who we are meant to be, our calling. I'm sorry to be the one to break this news to you, but sometimes following your calling means you make less money. It's hard to make a choice between what we are designed to do and the amount of money we want to make, but making this choice will often show what we truly love.

Love is never driven by cost. Choosing less doesn't mean you are weak; sometimes it means you are strong enough to follow a vision of where you are going even when the decision is difficult. Warren Buffett said, "The difference between successful people and very successful people is that very successful people say 'no' to almost everything."[2] We say no to many things in order to say yes to what we love.

What do your debit card, credit card, and investment statements show about who and what you love? How important is financial security to you and your family? How much money is enough? Are you ready to put your money where your heart is?

A LIFELONG LOVE

Have you ever had a friend who had a great idea? He is the friend who talks about it every time you see him for a few weeks and maybe even takes some steps toward action on the idea. However, he fails to fully see the idea through to completion. We have all experienced the boy who cried wolf. The world is full of passionate people with ideas that could really change things, but excitement does not automatically equate with love.

Occasionally we even get on board with an idea, seeing the huge potential for good, and disaster follows. The initial excitement wears off and the person fades away, leaving frustration and disappointment in the wake. Why? Because temporary passion is not the same as love. Think about the difference between liking something on Facebook or Instagram—we can like a hundred updates and pictures each time we log on—and actually starting a blog about something we are interested in. It's a matter of degree. When we enter a time of transition, this is the right time to ruthlessly examine which things we like (or "heart") and which things we love.

As I have observed and counseled a number of people interested in start-ups, a pattern has emerged that separates the temporarily excited from the persevering change agents. Those who have a clear connection between their life story and the change they want to make in their world generally persevere past the initial honeymoon stage. If there is not a past experience driving future ambition, the chance of bringing that idea to life is very small. In the pursuit of a dream, there ought to be a life experience that has shaped the part of your heart driving that dream. That same life experience gives firsthand wisdom, which shapes your unique contribution to this problem. Because you have lived through this experience and gained knowledge and understanding that others don't have, you have a deeper love that is required in order for the problem to be solved. When confrontation hits hard, the people who drive through are the ones whose personal story and heart-level connection push them through the challenge.

Without a deep love for some aspect of what we are creating or sharing about, chances are we will not follow through. We may like the idea or see an opportunity, but if the idea does not have a direct correlation with our own story, there is a good chance it's not a true love. On the other hand, when a great idea correlates with a personal story, the likelihood of bringing that idea to life significantly rises. Love leads to action. Love leads toward change. Love empowers us to make things different. Love lasts.

When you look over the length of your life, do you see a thread of continuity? Something that comes up over and over again that you have experienced? How has that shaped who and what you love?

I LOVE DOING GOOD

Esther is a humanitarian photographer who has traveled the world, capturing the stories of some of the most innovative problem-solving projects of our time.[3] She has a unique ability to share the stories of people in developing nations with great dignity, hope, and possibility. I had the pleasure to hear her share with me how she approaches her work. She strives to not take photos of people without knowing their names and getting their permission first. She knows her subjects' names because she views each piece of her work as more than a photo; it's a person who is loved. Every photo should have a name, "because who we are is not our circumstances." She has traveled all over the world capturing moments of hope with people in the most difficult circumstances, and she lets them shine in galleries across the world.

Esther also shared a tension she often feels as she travels. Inevitably in places of need, a bus shows up with a group of people on a short-term mission trip. What catches her off guard is that the minute these people step off the bus they are snapping photos without restraint. She contemplated for a while doing a photojournalism project of this phenomenon: people taking pictures of people they have never met.

Her question about this behavior startled me: "Do you think these people are more interested in meeting the people, serving their needs, and caring for others' lives, or updating their Facebook status with the photo they just took of their mission endeavor?" As an observer in those moments, she has wrestled with the reality that though the visitors probably have good intentions, those intentions get lost in their quest to amplify the good behavior. And ultimately the visitors may cause more harm than good as many innocent people are not given a choice in whether or not their photographs are broadcast to the world.

Doing good has become a trait of my generation. Good works today are celebrated, shared, liked, promoted, followed, screen printed, funded, documented, photographed, profited from, volunteered on behalf of, strategized, and postured. Doing good has become amplified in a digital era as a way to be noticed.

Many of the good works we are engaged in are done with good motives and ought to be celebrated. We are made to love well and do good and encourage others to do the same. We live in a broken world, this is not how creation was intended to be, and we feel a deep desire to make things better. The reason I desire to do good is because I want to show an outward expression of my faith. Paul said in Ephesians 2:10, "For we are His workmanship, created in Christ Jesus for good works" (NKJV). In community, I desire to encourage others to do good works: "And let us consider how we may spur one another on toward love and good deeds" (Heb. 10:24). We are made to change what is broken through an outward expression of love. My friends and I often have deep connections with God in moments of doing good.

But as quickly as we can have a spiritual experience through doing good, our motives can shift in an instant. Sometimes our motives get shaped in directions that were not the original design. Am I loving people, or am I loving the idea of doing good? Do I desire the best for each person I come in contact with, or do I desire to feel the best about myself for the good I am doing? I have experienced this shift in my own motives through the publicity of our good works. Sometimes good works are not intended to be promoted. I have wrestled with trying to solve problems and wanting to be known for this good work. I need to question my motives: Is this for the good of others, or is it making me look and feel good? Is the story shared mostly focused on me? Who should be in the spotlight instead of me?

LOVE WHO FIRST

Love gets harder when we get honest. True maturity means that day after day we wrestle with whom we really love and whom we love most. Times of transition and tension offer us opportunities to ask these heart questions. There are things we love and things we want to love for all sorts of reasons. We will never love others fully if we love ourselves more. To understand whom and what we love, we must begin with self-reflection.

If I am truthful, my greatest tension in determining whom I love is my tendency to put myself before others. This is an unfortunate reality. Do I love anything or anyone more than myself? Do you love anything or anyone more than yourself? Whom you love most will gain priority in every choice. This is the deepest question in every decision.

My heart is revealed when I make choices in direct contrast to the things I say I love. Selfishness is the greatest battle for every love. Love on paper is easy to prioritize. Love in daily life shows our answers. For deeper love to drive choices that take us to our intended design, we must first engage our struggle with selfishness. This is the issue I least desire to confront, but it drives all decision making.

At the core of my existence, in my fallen state, I am a very selfish being. But I don't want to be selfish. Sometimes I look at what others are doing and saying and think they are wrong. If they are wrong, then I am right, and I want to tell them so in order to feel better about myself. I quickly learned this in the first year of marriage, when too often I chose myself over my wife. Me before we.

Selfishness shows its ugly head in seemingly insignificant things during those early marriage years. Andre and I love to sit down with newly married couples over a meal, especially those who have been married for about four to six months. Every couple has at least one story (funny in hindsight) about the tensions of living together that are rooted in selfish acts that drive the other person crazy. Toilet seats left up, toothpaste tops left off, and how much gasoline is enough to keep in the car tank regularly come up. Regardless of the example, the root is always the contrast between newlywed bliss and self-centered behavior. How these small issues are resolved, who gives up what, and the attitude with which the compromise happens often give me a glimpse of what that marriage will look like over the long run.

I started our marriage driving Andre crazy because I never closed the shower curtain after a shower, which I learned (though not quickly enough) creates mold on the shower curtain. Even worse than this, I used to put my wet towel on the bed while I was getting dressed *and* she was still in bed. Not a good combination. But Andre had some faults as well. Because she doesn't like to hear the ding of the microwave, she always stops it two seconds before the time runs out, so the microwave clock never shows the actual time. We drove each other crazy in those first few months until we talked about our faults and made simple changes to habits on behalf of our love. We chose to change how we lived for the person we loved.

Below the surface, selfishness pervades our minds and our actions. We want to love others more than ourselves, but in daily life the tension is difficult to live out. We want to be gracious. We want to be giving. We want to be encouraging. We want to be forgiving. We want to see the best in others. We want to platform the greatness of others. We want to share others' skills more than ours.

To make better choices, we need to change ourselves to move love from me to others. This is difficult. But may I encourage you that difficult does not mean worse. It often means better. Those things that are truly worth something are worth the fight to get to them. The hardest-fought accomplishments are the ones that mean the most. Therefore, we must share our most vulnerable selves with others, opening up broadly to reveal ourselves, knowing that it can be painful but also knowing that the alternative is worse.

C. S. Lewis talked about the opportunity and vulnerability of love:

> To love at all is to be vulnerable. Love anything, and your heart will certainly be wrung and possibly be broken. If you want to make sure of keeping it intact, you must give your heart to no one, not even to an animal. Wrap it carefully round with hobbies and little luxuries; avoid all entanglements; lock it up safe in the casket or coffin of your selfishness. But in that casket—safe, dark, motionless, airless— it will change. It will not be broken; it will become unbreakable, impenetrable, irredeemable.[4]

Opening yourself to others will always create tensions, but to never love creates loneliness and wishing for something more. Brené Brown expanded on C. S. Lewis's thoughts:

> Owning our story can be hard but not nearly as difficult as spending our lives running from it. Embracing our vulnerabilities is risky but not nearly as dangerous as giving up on love and belonging and joy—the experiences that make us the most vulnerable. Only when we are brave enough to explore the darkness will we discover the infinite power of our light.[5]

And she shared further:

> We cultivate love when we allow our most vulnerable and powerful selves to be deeply seen and known, and when we honor the spiritual connection that grows from that offering with trust, respect, kindness and affection. Love is not something we give or get; it is something that we nurture and grow, a connection that can only be cultivated between two people when it exists within each one of them—we can only love others as much as we love ourselves.[6]

You will not fully understand your love until you have dealt with yourself in relation to that love. To love others, you must value yourself enough to understand that you need others. Decisions that focus only on self-love will leave you unfulfilled.

Love is the root feeling and action required to making any choice that will have a significant long-term implication. There was a time when I thought love would overcome selfish ambition, but now I think that love gives us the *chance* to overcome selfish ambition. It is love that straightens out our selfishness and brings us closer to community. What you choose will show what you love. It is easy to say what you love, but actions determine true love. May love always drive our choices.

LOVE AS COMPETITION

As if it were not hard enough to discover what and whom we love, while coming to grips with how we love ourselves, the next tension comes when our loves compete. I love Jesus. I love my family. I love my work. I love pursuing my entrepreneurial dream. I love to help others. I love to provide financially for my family so we can travel and have a home with a dog and eat at tasty restaurants and generously contribute to the needs of others, so my daughter can go to dance class and I can see a Broadway show and on and on and on. Which love wins? God? Wife? Children? Dreams? Money? Work? Friends? Me?

What happens when two of the choices are in stark contrast to one another? What do I do then? What about when my wife's love impacts my love? What happens when her love challenges my time? Or when our dreams are given more love than our relationship? Would I be willing to work less to let her live her dream? What happens when my dreams and her dreams are in conflict? How does love affect these decisions? How do we pick one? Love in the broad perspective seems beautiful and simple. But in the details love ultimately has competition. How do we choose what we love most, and how do we respond to that tension in community?

These moments of tension are the hardest to process. When we are forced to decide between two options that are both lovely, one love will always trump another. Sometimes our love and dreams clash, increasing tension and confusion. Unfortunately there is no formula to figure these moments out.

In the second half of this book, I will share six key elements of a process for thinking through these moments when we don't know what to do, elements that have worked as guides in my relationships. But if you are looking for immediate direction for what to do when multiple loves are competing, consider prioritizing your loves. People don't often do this on paper, yet we are forced to set priorities in our commitments of time and money. Your calendar and budget spell out your priorities.

So write out your greatest loves on a piece of paper. Put a number next to each love—rank them. Ask a friend to go through the process with you; your friend's responsibility is to not let you give an equal ranking to any two different loves. Choose one order. Then see how your life matches the priorities on your paper.

There are two things I do know about these moments. First, if *what* you love too often takes priority over *whom* you love, you will have no cause for celebration. I personally believe the people we love should be more important than any project. Second, when we notice a moment when our loves are in conflict, it is a sign to stop and process our priorities. Often we have not properly prioritized our loves or we have not acted on our priorities. Something must change, and it is our responsibility to stop and reflect upon what is happening to our loves and what love we value most.

These love-versus-love conflicts occur in very practical moments of tension all the time. It is common to see them played out in balancing work and family. Do I go to my daughter's dance recital or to the meeting with a new potential client? Do I look at my email, or do I build blocks with my little boy? Do I invest money in a new idea or work to pay off our family credit card bill? We make decisions every day about whom and what we love. It is vital to see the significance of each one.

Most of our greatest tensions involve putting aside self-love and sharing vulnerably while balancing the needs, dreams, expectations, and desires of all those we love. Pursuing what we love with the ones we love is a beautiful mix of saying yes and no. It often requires slowing down to work through the differences, the misunderstandings, and the mistakes. When we are in the middle of the hard times that inevitably come, having those we love supporting us and digging in with us is often our lifeline. Nothing compares to reaching the finish line hand in hand with the ones we love, all sharing the glory, the joy, and the deep sense of accomplishment of a life well lived … together. If we gain the world and lose those we love, we've lost.

LOVE AS CAREER OR SIDELINE

As we dig deeper into major life choices, identifying and prioritizing love will start to burn another question into our hearts: Is what we love also the work we should pursue? Don't we all wish we could read a book that would answer that question for us? Sadly, a book cannot give you *your* yes or no. This question requires significant time to process. One thing I know: understanding what and whom you love is only one component of what you are made to do. This question is complex and also unique to each individual. You may find love in your work, or like Brett and Garrick, you may keep your work separate from your love and still find a creative outlet to express your love. Love is just one piece of the picture.

Another piece of the picture is our story. All of who we are up to this point should significantly influence our future choices. Let's move on to curating our lives in a way that both honors and continues what we have experienced up to this point.

TAKE ACTION

Whom do you love? What do you love? When we are pondering what to do when we don't know what to do, the starting place is determining our love and how this moment of choice will affect that love. Until you have clarity in love, it will be difficult to become a decision maker.

Whom do you love and what do you love? Whom and what do you want to love more? Write them down. On paper. Consider how you will need to live differently to make decisions that choose those loves over self. How will that show up in the money and time you spend?

Other desires may try to take you away from what you truly desire to love, so make sure you write down those also. The quickest path to who you were made to be will be a line toward your true loves. Prioritize your love. Make sure what and whom you love are shown in your daily life.

QUESTIONS FOR GROUPS

1. How does knowing what and whom you love help you make good decisions?
2. What does your calendar reveal about what and whom you love? What does your checkbook reveal? Do you wish that picture looked different? If so, how?
3. What are some ways in which the things and people you love can compete with each other? How do you prioritize?

4

LIFE CURATED

What Wisdom Do You Have?

Knowledge is horizontal, but wisdom is
vertical—it comes down from above.
Billy Graham

I had reached the line for the first time in my life. That line that opened my world to new possibilities, new heights, new fears, and screaming like I had never before screamed. You know the line I'm talking about: the line on a vertical stick with a magic number. The line that determines if you are in or out. Yes or no. The line that determines if you are tall enough to ride the best rides—the roller-coaster line! Forty-eight inches. Four feet tall. *Yes!*

It seemed like it took forever to reach that line. How many times had I run up to the stick, thrown my shoulders back, and slyly inched up on tiptoe, trying to reach the magic line? Finally, the day arrived.

My head reached the line! My dad and I were overjoyed. It was Space Mountain at Disneyland, and we were ready to ride it together. A father-and-son moment to remember forever.

Together, we entered a small spaceship about to take off for the moon. On this indoor roller coaster, the lights were dim but the atmosphere was electric. Dad sat in back with me right in front of him. I held on tightly to the railings on either side of me, and Dad's hands were right on top of mine. The spaceship took off. It was amazing. Wind was blowing through my hair and fluorescent lights were zooming by in every direction. For some reason, I noticed Dad's grip tightening a little at every turn. I started yelling, trying to get my dad to loosen his grip, but thinking I was scared, he yelled back, "I got you, Jeff; don't worry!"

"Dad!" I wasn't screaming for my life, or even excitement; I was screaming because I had no feeling in my fingers. Each time we hit another twist or turn, he gripped tighter and tighter and tighter. To make matters worse, he was sporting a gold '80s-style ring as big as his knuckle on one of his fingers. When we stepped out of the spaceship, I had a welt on my hand from that ring pressing into my hand harder and harder and harder. If I look carefully in the right light, I think I can still see the marks on my hand.

Even on a wild and crazy roller coaster, it is the unplanned and unexpected that makes a mark. Oddly enough, it is those very unexpected scars that lead to wisdom. Wisdom doesn't happen in a day; wisdom is gained with every day. Wisdom is not an achievement; it is one way we learn to live, built upon our experiences. Every experience, however unexpected, offers us the chance to accumulate the wealth of wisdom.

Whenever I go to amusement parks now, I am always with a group of friends. Experiencing the thrill of the adventure is "better together."[1] Also, waiting in line with friends makes the time go by faster. The typical waiting line conversations usually start with catching up on life—job, family, hobbies. They usually involve sharing embarrassing moments and other doubling-over-in-laughter stories. Next come the conversation games requiring words and some creativity. My personal favorite is Would You Rather? Each round takes only a few minutes, so it tends to pop up over and over again throughout a day. Would You Rather? is based on hypothetical but over-the-top situational choices. The hilarity ensues when someone has to choose one of two outrageous and often cringe-inducing options.

Would you rather choose to smash grapes with your feet until they turned into wine or lick the bottom of your boyfriend's feet after he walked around the amusement park all day in sandals?

Would you rather swim with sharks at feeding time or have your hand stuck inside a bees' nest for thirty minutes?

Would you rather eat only gummy worms for the rest of your life or be forced to never eat the same thing twice, ever?

Rounds of this game are actually the first clear memories I have of thinking through decisions. It may seem weird, but I think processing these extreme choices set me up to tackle decisions that others don't want to make. For me, these silly games prepared me for future choices. Working through a more ridiculous situational option makes everyday decision making seem simpler. These game scenarios will never be reality, but they get us thinking in new ways and cause us to think hard about what we will do when we don't know what to do. It's the start of our decision-making journey.

We all have past experiences that drive what we think today and how we will make decisions for our future. Wisdom happens through the experiences that have made us who we are and what we will become. This is our life story—how we choose to curate that story makes up a major portion of our decision-making style and what we determine is wise.

I used to think that being wise was only equated with getting old, just a higher level on that stick at the entrance of each roller coaster. Since wisdom would only be found through longevity, it felt like an out-of-reach virtue. In order to gain wisdom from others, I would have to set up meetings with the elderly and listen and learn.

I was wrong. Wisdom increases with life experience. You don't suddenly become wise at a certain age. And just being old does not mean you are a sage. Wisdom doesn't just happen along the road. It is something to pursue.

SWEATPANTS AND PROVERBS

Dr. Gayle D. Beebe is the president of Westmont College and studied under Peter Drucker, one of the greatest organizational minds of our time who shaped business as we know it through his writings. When I was twenty years old, Dr. Beebe was the president of the university I attended. I checked my email one afternoon to find a message from Dr. Beebe asking to meet.

I first said yes, because what other option was there? Then I started freaking out about what I may have done wrong. He suggested we meet at his house at 10:00 p.m. The president of my school, whom I had only seen wearing full suits and ties, was asking me to meet with him at his house late in the evening. I wondered if he would be wearing a suit at that time of day because that was the only way I could picture him, as if he had no other kinds of clothes. I decided to wear jeans and a button-down shirt. He told me that his kids would already be in bed and that I was to enter through a specific side door and he would meet me in the den. It was beginning to sound like a secret society invitation.

I walked in the door, and he was sitting in an oversized chair with a fireplace blazing behind him. The room was surrounded by books and gave me the sense that we were surrounded by hundreds of years of others' knowledge. He quickly stood up and welcomed me into his home. He was wearing gray cotton sweatpants and a sweatshirt featuring his favorite football team. For some reason, I had never imagined him in anything other than a suit. I remember telling him this perception, and we both laughed uproariously about the truth of the matter, because if he had a choice he would be playing sports every day in sweatpants and a T-shirt.

Dr. Beebe was purposeful and quickly moved the conversation toward how he desired to mentor me throughout my time in college. I have since realized that wise people have a way of directing a conversation to lead people toward new thinking. He was dropping wisdom on me that night, and all I could do was begin note taking.

We got together monthly and followed a simple plan. I could ask him questions about leadership and calling. He would share something with me that he knew I needed to understand. Over the years of his mentorship, he caught me doing good things and found out about many of my worst mistakes. The amazing thing was that even after bad choices, we still got together and talked through life. He sat with me, as wise leaders ought to do, through the highs and lows. I think he knew that most of our greatest mistakes build into us our greatest wisdom.

Dr. Beebe taught me to pursue wisdom rather than wait for it to happen to me. He set up an intentional process by which I could question and learn and he could share what he knew with the younger generation. We find wisdom when we pursue it.

He also gave me a specific path by which to acquire wisdom. During one of our first meetings, he shared with me the greatest advice he felt he had ever received: read Proverbs every day. A small-*p* proverb is simply a short truth or piece of advice. Most every ancient and modern culture passes proverbs down through generations. But the capital-*P* Proverbs Dr. Beebe shared with me is found in the Bible. The book of Proverbs, written mostly by Solomon, is filled with collections of practical wisdom. Since there are at most thirty-one days in a month and Proverbs has thirty-one chapters, it is a simple practice to open to the chapter that coincides with the day and read. So much wisdom that we need as problem solvers and decision makers is found in this book of wisdom. A chapter from Proverbs a day guides your choices in good ways.

Proverbs begins with a premise and a promise: seeking wisdom leads you down the right road.

> My son, if you accept what I am telling you
> and store my counsel and directives deep
> within you,

If you listen for Lady Wisdom, attune your ears to
her,
and engage your mind to understand what she
is telling you,
If you cry out to her for insight
and beg for understanding,
If you sift through the clamor of everything around
you
to seek her like some precious prize,
to search for her like buried treasure;
Then you will grasp what it means to truly respect
the Eternal,
and you will have discovered the knowledge of
the one True God.
The Eternal is ready to share His wisdom with us,
for His words bring true knowledge and insight;
He has stored up the essentials of sound wisdom for
those who do right;
He acts as a shield for those who value integrity.
God protects the paths of those who pursue justice,
watching over the lives of those who keep faith
with Him.
With this wisdom you will be able to choose the
right road,
seek justice, and decide what is good and fair
Because wisdom will penetrate deep within
and knowledge will become a good friend to
your soul.

Sound judgment will stand guard over you,
>> and understanding will watch over you as the
>> Lord promised.
Wisdom will keep you from following the way of
>> evildoers,
>> of those who twist words to pervert the truth,
Of those who reject the right road
>> for a darker, more sinister way of life,
Of those who enjoy evil
>> and pursue perverse pleasures,
Of those who journey down a crooked path,
>> constantly figuring out new ways to trick and
>> deceive others....
As for you, you should walk like those who are good
>> and keep to the paths of those who love
>> justice,
For those who live right will remain in the land
>> and those with integrity will endure here.
>> (Prov. 2:1–15, 20–21 VOICE)

When we seek out wisdom, not only will we find wisdom, we will also find the source of all wisdom, God Himself. When we find the all-knowing God and continue to seek the knowledge and discernment that come only from Him, not only will we choose the right paths, but we will find the strength to endure there. And tucked into all of this right-path finding is the beautiful realization that not only is it the right path for us but it is a path of justice for others.

SEEKING GOD

I know that not every person reading this may share my faith, but for me, the starting place to gain wisdom is through the pursuit of God. I believe the greatest wisdom is found in God Himself. The more we pursue God, the more clarity will be released into our minds and choices. Many people can speak wisdom into your life, but only One knows what has happened, what is happening, and what is going to happen: the all-knowing, all-seeing God. I find it interesting that as we pursue wisdom and justice and right paths, Proverbs 2 tells us that eventually those paths will lead us to God. I have witnessed firsthand those steps toward God in others' stories.

I had a conversation with a friend recently about a Kickstarter project he was launching. He had everything ready—a sweet video, awesome perks, and a project that was truly worth funding. Everything was ready, he had written the email, and then he stopped. Though my friend has wrestled all his life with the idea of whether or not God even exists, he and I continually discuss my faith and how I believe that God knows, cares, and is an active part of the day-to-day affairs of this world. He said just before he pushed the final button, he prayed. He said in that moment something in him realized that all the hard work he had done was officially out of his control once it was time to share it with the world. He said he wasn't really expecting God to intervene in this situation, but in his words, it was at least worth a shot. Something in him knew that as much as he was not God, there just might be Someone who was.

Moments of transition or tension often lead us to the knowledge of our own limits and the recognition that we need help from beyond ourselves. I think we instinctively know, or at least hope, that there is something bigger than us, Someone who is for us and behind us. We desire the reassurance that things will be okay. We sense in moments of tension that there might be one person who sees the future, and we want a glimpse of that wisdom. This is our opportunity to connect with the source of wisdom.

Sadly, many people want to use God as a consultant on retainer whom they can phone whenever they need advice but otherwise ignore in their daily lives. This is not the way to a life of wisdom. In Proverbs 2, Solomon spoke of calling out and crying aloud, searching as for hidden treasure. He was describing a persistent, habitual pursuit of wisdom in our daily lives. I believe seeking the knowledge, understanding, and wisdom that can come only from God should be the starting, ongoing, and ending points for all decisions.

Knowledge can be found in a myriad of places. As a follower of Jesus, I start by finding life-changing knowledge in the Bible. Through reading Scripture, I consistently gain the knowledge of what is true from a heavenly perspective instead of only a personal or cultural perspective. As I read of the decisions that others made, the ways they made them, and the consequences of their decisions, I find not only direction for my own life but an understanding of why we are where we are today.

For instance, the first major decision humans made was in the Garden of Eden, when Adam and Eve chose to eat from the one tree God told them not to eat from (Gen. 3). They chose to go against a specific direction from God. Can you imagine making one choice and having every single woman in history blame you for pain during childbirth? At least none of my choices will lead to brokenness for all mankind. That is not to minimize the complexity of our decisions, but Adam and Eve made a wrong choice that had pretty big implications.

Or consider the decision-making process Noah endured in choosing to make the ark. He received a vision from God that made no sense to the people of his time, yet for years he pursued his commitment to see it through to completion. The Bible is filled with story after story of decisions being made. Even studying how the Scriptures were written informs and inspires my pursuit of wisdom: Paul wrote at least eleven books of the New Testament while in prison. When I was in Rome, I had the opportunity to visit one of the prisons Paul wrote from, and his choices became real in a completely new way. When we know our path is God directed, we will persevere.

I often return to a reading of Matthew, Mark, Luke, and John to see once again the life of Jesus that I may learn from the ultimate example of following God's direction. From the age of twelve all the way to His gut-wrenching decision to die on the cross, Jesus's life was defined by His decision to follow His purpose to be about His Father's work. He made choices to heal the sick, stand up against religious rulers, eat and drink with swindlers and prostitutes, and share His wisdom with all who would listen. He chose a group of twelve close friends and encouraged all to live a new story.

As we move forward on the path God has for each of us, I can't state strongly enough that true wisdom comes with seeking God, not self. This wisdom then provides a lens through which we can curate our lives. We develop the insight required to look back over our experience and glean wisdom for our future. As we listen to the wisdom shared by others, we have a filter to recognize what knowledge is true and what is false. We develop the kind of sight that finds the paths most helpful to seeking justice for our world in ways that honor God and people. We become wise.

FIND KNOWLEDGE

We also find knowledge for our particular journey through two different mediums—experience and academics. Experiential knowledge is the process of learning from the stories of our lives. Academic knowledge is learning from others through reading, listening, and researching the stories of experts and practitioners. By combining these two spheres of learning, we fill up a bank of knowledge from which we can draw in our ongoing decision making. This is the kind of bank account that is meant to grow daily. Our knowledge enlarges from a life lived and learned.

Life Lived

What is your earliest childhood memory? From our first memory and even earlier, we have been building a bank of knowledge through simply living life. We each have a story that we live out every day. We remember our first kiss, the coaches who taught us a game, the time we put our foot in our mouth at the wrong moment, and a host of other experiences that make up who we are today. Life experience teaches us plenty; some good things, some sad, many regrets, unrepeatable events, and moments that bring great clarity to life. Experience gives us memories and crafts our future. Experiential knowledge is the process of being educated through the collection of stories through which we have lived.

Our past stories play a major component in who we are becoming. I think sometimes we wish we could erase our past, literally clear our history. But it's not possible. I've done many things that I wish I could take back. My mom always says, "God never wastes experiences." All the pieces of our lives, good and bad, can be used for our purposeful walking in the journey ahead. The key is not to be defined by the past but to be formed by it. Take the knowledge you have learned and use it to shape who you are becoming.

Life Learned

Andre walked into the house one day to find me reading a book on marriage. It was clear that she was not impressed. "Why are you reading that?" she asked. (Note that we both tend to be brutally honest and enjoy giving each other a hard time.)

I was reading a book on marriage written by a woman who had been divorced and was now remarried. Because of the controversy surrounding this fact, Andre perceived the book as not worth reading. I responded, "I'm reading a book about marriage and you're giving me a hard time?" She kind of laughed and said, "Good point."

We went on to have a great conversation. The truth is that if I'm reading a book about marriage, the chances are high that it will help my marriage. Regardless of the premise or approach, it is likely I can find a way to learn something, apply it, and benefit my marriage. Every book, every talk, every story has the potential to teach me one new thing to put in my pocket of life knowledge. Tim Keller once said, "When you listen and read one thinker, you become a clone … two thinkers, you become confused … ten thinkers, you'll begin developing your own voice … two or three hundred thinkers, you become wise and develop your voice." Academic knowledge happens through learning from others, through reading, listening to, and researching the stories of others.

I believe we can learn something from everyone. Regardless of their philosophical approach, political view, ideology, theology, strategy, passion, or purpose, I can still learn something from others. As my friend Lisa always says, "Eat the fish and spit out the bones." The more we learn from others, the broader view we will have. They may be younger, older, less educated, or more thoughtful—we have the opportunity to take one new thought away from every person we interact with. Even if we don't agree with them, we can gain insight into other ways of thinking, choosing, and living.

I have been having more and more conversations with people who are offended that I integrate unlikely individuals' thoughts into my psyche; they think it may be dangerous. I hear statements like: "Why would you quote them?" "How could you read their book?" "You listen to that person?" "I can't believe you would even give them your time." But is it right that we would disregard people completely simply because we don't agree with them completely? Is it possible that we don't want to have to do the work of discerning what is right or wrong about what they might be saying? Are we taking the easy way out by casting them aside completely? Every person has broken-ness in his or her life, myself included. If they have acquired wisdom in the midst of their brokenness, then I should listen. We all make choices that not everyone else would agree with.

Why does this matter?

First, it matters because of the connectedness of ideas. In *The Tipping Point*, Malcolm Gladwell referred to a unique type of person he called a Maven. Mavens are "information specialists," or "people we rely on to connect us with new information." I believe if we are moving forward in society with the pursuit of innovation, taking information from a wide array of thought, and connecting this thinking together, we will create the future of innovation. Knowledge from chefs, environmental activists, educators, and accountants comes together at the perfect time to make something new that will change life as we know it. Understanding what is coming will give us time to process how to respond in a thoughtful way.

Too often we hear something and think there is no benefit for our future in this information, yet we could be missing out on an opportunity to expand our mind on this topic. The people who can connect ideas from seemingly disparate places will create what is common for tomorrow. The bringing together of utterly impossible ideas into something that does not now exist is where brilliance emerges. The more informed we are, the greater choices we will make.

Second, a greater view leads to deeper creation. The way I see the world is often limited to my experiences. When I experience and learn from others' knowledge, my breadth of worldview extends further. My story is very small in the context of the broad world, and I want to understand the world in a greater way. In the pursuit of innovation, the more we know, the more informed creators we become. If I have a limited view of the world, this causes a limited view of what I have the potential to create. By learning from others, I will gain a greater perspective.

Third, learning sets us apart. The truth is, most people don't take the time to keep learning. If you had the privilege of attending college, there is a good chance you heard professors talk about the importance of being a lifelong learner. Too many people don't take this seriously. This does not mean they don't have the books—it is very common for organizational leaders to have the books on their bookcases, but it is also very common that the books have never been cracked open, let alone read. Continuing to learn and looking for ways to diversify learning are instant differentiators in any marketplace.

You may feel uncomfortable with my call to wider learning. While I don't ask that you agree, I would like you to consider one takeaway. Next time you find yourself in a place to hear the story or teaching of a person to whom you generally would not give the time of day, try something for me. Stop evaluating what you hear in terms of what you don't agree with. Instead, focus on one question: What is one thing I can take away from what this person is saying? Just one thing. Try to learn one thing. The speaker may not see the world the way you do. That's okay—actually, that's the point. We all have something to learn from one another.

Academic knowledge is the active process of research with the hope of understanding more. I believe that the more we learn, the wiser the choices we have the potential to make.

LIVE THE LEARNING

From the knowledge we have gained from our lives lived and lessons learned from others, it is our responsibility to apply what we learn thoughtfully. I know how to eat healthfully. I know that if I work out every day, I will feel better and my body will get stronger. I know that eating dessert is probably not good for me. So, do I eat healthfully every day? Do I work out consistently? Do I eat dessert? How often do I apply the knowledge directly to my life? Just because we know something doesn't mean we have changed our lives to understand it and apply it to daily life.

Albert Einstein pointedly said, "Any fool can know. The point is to understand." Through technology, we have information shooting at us every moment of every day. There is no shortage of information. Even when we don't know something, we can find it out in a matter of seconds. "Google it" is the common phrase we use.

I was recently in a meeting with some venture capital investors, and they were talking about a word I had never heard before and truthfully didn't understand. Like any good professional trying to look engaged, I was nodding my head in agreement as they talked, while pretending to take notes on my phone. I was actually looking up the word, trying to understand the dialogue to be able to stay part of the conversation. Knowledge is at our fingertips. The question becomes, what will we do with this abundance of information?

Curators are people who care for something. It is a title most commonly used for the person in charge of a museum. Curators take pride in finding the best items to present and the best places to present them. They are decision makers sorting through everything at their disposal to feature a few things. Applying understanding forces people to become curators of the abundance of knowledge, sorting through all the knowledge they have, applying it in the right places and at the right times. Once we begin to find God's wisdom, discern the significance of our own experiences, and gather knowledge from others, we have the tools to curate life in a meaningful way.

Jeremy Blume is the cofounder of Bearings, "a biweekly guide and shop that points men toward a well-rounded life by connecting them to intriguing, enriching, and uncommon aspects of culture, food, drink, attire, music, home, knowledge, travel, and the outdoors."[2] Jeremy often takes time to reflect on what he is learning and think about how to apply what matters most. He said,

> We are personally responsible for the safeguarding of our lives and we choose how we make the most of it.
>
> A key part of living like a curator is defining what's valuable to you. We learn and refine this over time, but it needs to be a way of life and a process of thinking.… Life is a prized collection, make it unique and make the most of it.[3]

In order to become decision makers, we must take the things we learn (knowledge) and apply them to life. We take the story we have lived and the information we have gleaned and apply that understanding in a way that leads us to action that counts.

TRANSLATING WISDOM

Andre grew up in Bolivia, the daughter of missionaries. Her first language was Spanish, and it brings us great joy to travel to Spanish-speaking communities. It usually takes her some time to pick back up her native language, but she is still bilingual. I know enough Spanish to understand directions, buy what I need, and order off a menu. Needless to say, I prefer to use Andre to translate what needs to be communicated, and I feel confident in a Spanish-speaking area when I know she is with me.

Wisdom is much like the process of translation. Wisdom is the translation of knowledge and understanding in order to apply them within others' lives. You will know you are a person of wisdom when others ask for your advice in their moments of tension and transition. We may not think of ourselves as wise because we always consider another person wiser. That might be called humility. However, if we have been living a life that seeks God, searches for knowledge, and works toward understanding, we will gain wisdom. Wisdom is the mix of experience, knowledge, and good judgment, along with the ability to translate that information to transform others' life experiences. Whether or not you think of yourself as wise, if others are asking your opinion, they probably think of you as a wise person. Wisdom is a beautiful gift you can share with others. It is taking your curated knowledge and applying it to the struggles and questions of others. Wisdom that is not shared is not wise at all.

Bob Briner's book *Roaring Lambs* introduced me to a concept that has imprinted on my life: that we need to "earn the right to be heard." Once we live lives of purpose, seeking wisdom ourselves, living lives of love for others, sharing who we are, we open up the possibility of sharing our wisdom. We earn the right to be heard. When you have walked in steps that others have not, they will ask for your advice.

For me, it started with a few simple emails from friends who wanted me to meet with another person about some random ideas they were working on. I have started many projects that are atypical and are considered by others as social enterprises. As others were embarking in this space, our mutual friends would introduce me and ask me to speak into their projects. We would go have a cup of coffee and they would share their ideas. They wanted my advice. I wouldn't say that in every scenario I gave the greatest wisdom, but I tried to translate any wisdom from my understanding that I could give. Over time I realized that these were incredible opportunities to discern and speak humbly. And I recognized that my life experience has given me wisdom to share.

This idea of sharing wisdom developed into building an entire education arm of our organization. Through our Plywood Retreats, I have had the opportunity to speak into eighty different start-up ideas that seek to solve problems in the world. Recently, we gathered all of them together for a lunch. After we started the lunch, I sat in the corner and looked around at the joy on every person's face. I got up, left my plate of food sitting on the table, walked to the bathroom, and looked in the mirror. I could not believe that God had used me in this way to serve all these people. Many people are wiser than I am, yet these people found wisdom in my words. When you get the opportunity to speak into another person's story, remember the gift that has been entrusted to you. Give freely, because someone has equally shared with you at some point.

This collection of wisdom gained in life must play a role in decision making. You have been given this information for a reason. What you love mixed with your life story will line up with what you will be known for and will come together to create your philosophy of choice.

WORDS OF WISDOM

Several years ago, three of my new friends, Kerry, Erin, and Anne, invited my wife and me to a birthday party. These three friends have toured the world together, and we all met through our church. The backyard was aglow beneath a canopy of white lights. These friends aren't halfhearted in their celebrations, and this particular theme party was a mishmash of Halloween, Mexican fiesta, and Hawaiian luau—in other words, everyone wore costumes while we limbo danced and drank margaritas. Sometime later in the evening, Kerry loudly called out, "Words of wisdom." Everyone immediately stopped whatever they were doing to give undivided attention to the celebrated birthday girl. Cameras started flashing, pens and papers prepared for recording, and the crowd waited. The birthday celebrant was to share with the community any words of wisdom she had learned in the last year.

Over the years, we've witnessed a full range of responses to this declaration, from clamming up and wanting to hide to carefully arranged declarations of wisdom. Most of us have particular moments that trigger us to reflect on what has happened. I often reflect during the time between Christmas and New Year's. But birthdays offer another clear moment of reflection. Over the last year of my life, what did I learn? The beauty of these "words of wisdom" stuns me every time. No one records the words for some kind of test; rather, they eagerly desire to learn from one another. Seeking, learning, applying, sharing, and curating the wisdom you possess—that is a life worth living and a decision worth choosing.

TAKE ACTION

Words of wisdom need not be saved for a holiday. Wisdom power is greatest when it is translated and shared with others. Next time you have a meal with friends, share your wisdom with each other. Talk to them about this idea, and ask everyone at the table to share one nugget of wisdom they have gained from the last year. If you do this, I promise everyone will walk away encouraged and wanting to know more about the wisdom that is deep within each other's souls. Begin the practice of gleaning and sharing wisdom from unexpected places.

QUESTIONS FOR GROUPS

1. What is one piece of wisdom you have gained in the past year?
2. The book of Proverbs urges us to search for wisdom like buried treasure. How can you do that? What role does God play in your pursuit of wisdom?
3. What does it mean to be a lifelong learner? What helps you do that? What gets in the way? What do you think of approaching every source with the question "What is one thing I can take away from what this person is saying?"

5

PROBLEM SOLVERS

What Will You Be Known For?

The one who sees the problem has the responsibility to fix it.
Simon Mainwaring

Mr. Rudd was my math teacher when I was in seventh grade. He had short red hair, glasses, and a tightly trimmed red beard. Every Wednesday we explored the "problem of the day." It was my favorite part of school on those days. The problem of the day was always a clever issue phrased in such a way as to trick us into an incorrect solution. Spotting the tricks and uncovering the real answer felt more like a game than math. If we got the answer right, we would get extra credit for the week. Little did I know that twenty years later I would still enjoy the game, that I would actually build my life around solving problems, but that is exactly what I get the opportunity to do.

A few years ago, Andre and I had a packed week of evening meetings. The first evening, we had dinner with another married couple. They opened up to us about some marriage issues they were having and asked for some advice. Now, our marriage isn't perfect in any way, but often we can share with others out of our failures and things we have learned along the journey of commitment.

The next evening, we went to our small group from church. We were the leaders of the group and stayed late into the night talking with a woman about how frustrated she was with her job and how she was wrestling with what to do with her life. We walked through a series of questions and tried to develop a plan of how she could move forward with transitioning into a new area of work.

The next morning, Andre went to work and had a team meeting with her coworkers about the transition of their technology system. Believe it or not, in 2010 they only then were upgrading from a DOS system to a Windows-based system. In the conversation, Andre made some targeted observations about what needed to happen and why. She walked out of the meeting with a new title and new responsibility: super-user and leader of the technology transition training for the rest of the team.

That same day, I had lunch with a friend who was launching a new business. He had an idea—but there were multiple holes in the idea. As I began poking at all the holes to try to make the idea better, he asked me to be an adviser on this project. In total, over about four days, Andre and I problem solved for a minimum of ten scenarios throughout our community.

During a car ride later that week, we debriefed these conversations. What we realized was that in every place we go, we find problems. We see what is broken. And we want to be part of fixing the situations. Those of us who are leaders solve problems instinctively; we see what others don't see. We see the path that restores what is broken. We see the possibilities of what could make things better. We feel responsible for making that happen. We want things to be right, and it frustrates us when something is not working the way it ought to be. We often step into scenarios where questions are left unanswered, and we push forward to a decision.

That car ride was a significant moment in both of our lives. We have always known we have the ability to lead, but we understood it in a different way through that conversation. When we as leaders start taking responsibility for problems we see, we turn into leaders of action—in short, problem solvers earning influence. We feel the need to make choices that others are not willing to make. Instead of simply having the ability to lead, we take responsibility and turn toward the act of decision making. By making decisions, we solve problems. We move from potential to action, from idea to implementation. That conversation caused us to realize that when we see problems, we feel a responsibility to fix them.

RESPONSIBILITY

We thought everyone felt that sense of responsibility, but not every person does have that yearning toward making things better. In fact, we noticed that many people run away from the burden of decision making, unwilling to take on the weight of responsibility and take ownership of the results.

Why do I push toward making decisions? I believe when we make choices, they lead us closer to making things more right than they are today. If I can make a dent toward progress, I feel a connection to why I exist; I find purpose in life. Who and what you love combined with your past story and wisdom will help you solve problems on the way toward your dreams. All this joined together gives you the opportunity to be known as a problem solver, through a life span of making daily decisions toward this purpose.

The tension in being a problem solver is that it never stops. We can be in a committee meeting at our daughter's preschool and see the problems. We get a tour through a new office with a friend and see all the things the company still needs to get set up. We walk through our neighborhood and see the trash and feel compelled to pick it up. We look for a house and see the things wrong and the potential of what it could be with some hard work. We go to another country and see extreme needs and want to be part of the solution. Problem solvers want to be part of the solution every place they go. It is the greatest opportunity that we have and the deepest challenge to manage. Now that we understand that about ourselves, we have the responsibility to determine our unique callings to the specific problems we are to join in solving.

PROBLEMS SOLVED, NOT AVOIDED

I believe there is a direct correlation between who we admire most in society and what choices they chose to make. Most often, they chose to do something that others would not have chosen. They were problem solvers. They chose to create new solutions to some of the world's greatest challenges. Rather than being content to sit back while yet another question lay unanswered, they brought innovative solutions to a major social problem. They were social innovators: people who chose to solve problems that no other person would address.

Social innovators are finding solutions and addressing the most pressing societal needs of our generation. When you think of one of these leaders, you instantly connect the name of the person with the problem he or she is solving. Let me give you a few examples.

Susan G. Komen: breast cancer
Blake Mycoskie: shoes
Scott Harrison: clean water
Gary Haugen: human trafficking
Jason Russell: Joseph Kony
Muhammad Yunus: microfinance
Martin Luther King Jr.: civil rights
Wendy Kopp: education

You may or may not agree with the importance of certain people's causes or the approaches they have chosen to take, but you know them by the problems they are addressing. Problem solvers don't just have résumés; they have stories of solutions that everyone can recite and celebrate. Those stories usually go back to a series of choices they made to pursue a problem they felt personally responsible to solve. You may not agree with the solution they have determined is right, but you understand that they are pursuing a problem and giving their lives to meeting a broken thing that needs to be fixed.

Plywood People promotes this simple mantra: "We will be known by the problems we solve." The city of Atlanta, where we live and serve, has had a difficult time finding its identity. I feel responsible to help find that solution. My vision is for Atlanta to be known over time as a center for social innovation. Social innovation is a strong component of our history. Martin Luther King Jr. pursued his vision for human rights from the heart of our city. Atlanta is also home to Coca-Cola, whose innovative business practices have not only changed the daily life of Americans but also traversed the globe. Plywood People seeks to utilize the best of both—to find innovative solutions to the world's most pressing needs. We hope to bridge the passion for human rights with the ideas of corporate innovation.

Through these last few years of sitting with social innovators, I have noticed an emerging theme. Whether these start-ups are for profit or not for profit, small scale or far-reaching, local or international, all of them are solving problems. As the title "social innovator" or "social entrepreneur" gains widened popularity, the people truly making a difference are not known by either amorphous title. If you claim to be one of these people, you are known by the change you are making in society. You are known by the problem you are solving. Your choices bend toward that solution. You say no to things that take you away from your cause. You say yes to things that bring you closer to your calling and responsibility. If you are an innovator, your name becomes synonymous with your solution. Until this happens, we are all just aspiring innovators. The story always leads you.

Most people flee problems. Problems frustrate. Problems stop people in their tracks. Problems throw up roadblocks that cause the people facing the problems to raise the white flag of surrender. But problem solvers have found another way to look at problems. Problems create a distraction from accomplishing something significant. Henry Ford explained it this way: "Most people spend more time and energy going around problems than in trying to solve them." When we hit a problem, we try to create a shortcut to keep moving, when in reality we have an incredible opportunity that is sitting in front of us: a problem needing to be solved. Most solutions begin with a choice to move toward a solution rather than avoid a problem or seek a way around it. When you line up a series of choices toward a solution, you will find a cause that will drive future decisions.

Innovators are the ones who attack, engage, experiment with, and ultimately solve problems in ways that have not been done previously. History remembers problem solvers because solving a problem literally changes the trajectory of the future. When a problem is solved, a new era begins. It was Albert Einstein who stated, "It's not that I'm so smart; it's just that I stay with problems longer."

Good ideas don't make a person known, though they may make the person appear unique or creative. Solving a problem plants a stake in history that can never be changed. We will be known by the problems we solve. Let's break this sentence down into its two distinct phrases.

TO BE KNOWN

The first element is the hope of being known. "Sometimes you want to go where everybody knows your name." This famous line of the theme song from the '80s hit sitcom *Cheers* speaks clearly the desire of a nation struck with loneliness. When your name is known and spoken, you feel a deep sense of self-worth, of identity. Americans have a strong attachment to names. Since Dale Carnegie hit the business world with *How to Win Friends and Influence People*, we have practiced remembering others' names because we know that makes them feel that they are important to us. A lot of people can know your name, however, without really knowing you. We all want to be known.

I struggle with this all the time. This morning I looked to see how many people were following me on Twitter. I often check to see if anyone liked my latest photo. Too often I try to quantify my influence, and then it becomes a ranking game of me versus the rest of the world. That's ridiculous. Why do I do these things that have no meaning?

Because I want to be known. I want to feel special, to feel loved, and to feel self-worth. I want people to think I matter. There is something within us that wants attention.

I have a friend named Mike. Mike has a truck, and everyone knows it. Thankfully Mike is generous with his truck, and he genuinely likes to help people. If you were moving and were friends with Mike, you would call him and ask to use his truck for your move. Mike has become known for having a truck and freely lending it to others when they need it. We all have a friend like Mike, or if we don't have one, we wish we did. We sit around on a couch, planning our big move—and what is the first problem we try to figure out? *Who has a truck?* We have a problem that needs to be solved. Mike has become known as a solution to that problem. Move. Truck. Mike. Solution.

We all want to be known; though not all of us want to be known the way Mike is known. We want to be known for making a Grammy Award–winning album. We want to be known as an amazing photographer. We want to be known as a successful entrepreneur. We want to be known as the writer of a clever Twitter statement that gets retweeted around the world. This selfish ambition drives an unimpressive passion for self-aggrandizement, and in an increasingly connected world, we have the outlet to pursue it. In our Twitter feed, Facebook posting, and Instagram posturing, we try to make ourselves look better than we truly are. Many cultural observers see this web-based quick route to fame leading to ever-increasing amounts of narcissism.

While I have also witnessed the rise of self-centered blogs, tweets, and posts, I wonder if both our desires to be known and the growing connectedness of the world can be used for good. Margaret Thatcher exclaimed years ago, "It used to be about doing something; now it's about being someone." I believe the future is about combining these pursuits. We have the potential to create solutions that are deeply significant and come from a person rooted in humility choosing the needs of others before self. A great modern example of this is Mother Teresa. She is known worldwide. Though she did most of her service before the Internet age, God led her to a problem to be solved, and forsaking all else, she solved that problem day after day. The world knew her and loved her for it.

Whether or not we use social tools, we are all known for something. Right now, you are known for something. I believe that if we could channel the desire to be known toward initiating common good ideas for people, the result would be better both for ourselves and for others. What are you currently known for? Reputation can be both from acts of kindness and goodness as well as from less desirable activities. Times of tension and transition offer us the chance to step back and seriously consider who we are, who others think we are, and who we hope to be.

While the Internet offers us easier ways to be known for something we are not, the fact is that this short-term veneer will never last. I encourage you to seek to be known for what only you can contribute to the world. Pursuing your calling as a problem solver is a gift to our world. What are you known for?

Interestingly, in moments of clarity most people have less desire to be known for accomplishments and more desire to be known for what kind of people they are. If someone stood to give a toast to you, what words would you want them to use to describe you? The words tend to lean toward character traits and values: *compassionate, generous, wise,* or maybe even *happy.* Maybe it is as simple as "good friend." A long-term view of what you want to be known for takes short-term achievement out of the equation and introduces virtues that have the power to radically redefine a life. Seasonal accolades become less valuable, replaced by a kind of lifestyle to pursue, a way to live life.

Problem solvers look to initiate good for the sake of others. Paul wrote it this way in Philippians 2:3–4: "Do nothing out of selfish ambition or vain conceit. Rather, in humility value others above yourselves, not looking to your own interests but each of you to the interests of the others." Whenever we prioritize the needs of others, our influence becomes stronger and more sincere. Prioritizing others will deepen the worth of your public identity. Being known may be a desire of many people, but when you prioritize making societal needs known, you simultaneously gain influence. You build a reputation that others respect and admire.

BE A PROBLEM SOLVER

Albert Einstein said, "The significant problems we face cannot be solved at the same level of thinking we were at when we created them." We all have dreams of becoming known for something significant. Problems are solved by having a dream and making decisions every day to pursue that dream. I have found there are four common practices that problem solvers choose.

1. Be in Places Where Problems Happen

Problem solvers spend time in places with problems. The more problems we see, the more we want to create solutions. If you claim to be a problem solver, but you never place yourself in proximity to problems, then you are just a problem talker. Go to where the problem is and dig in.

Leroy Barber, global executive director of Word Made Flesh,[1] taught me this in both word and action: "If you want to see beauty, you need to go to the darkest places on earth, and light will clearly shine." In the hardest places, we see the opportunity for the greatest potential. I believe some of the greatest innovations happen in the places and times of the greatest despair. Out of our suffering, solutions become clear. If we desire to create solutions, we need to go to the places of greatest need.

See the unseen need. Most people are inspired when they read or watch stories about people who solve problems. At times we all play a role of cultural commentator or consumer, but when you get a taste of being part of the solution, there is no turning back. Your life begins to move toward the problems instead of resisting the messiness experienced in the process.

Andre and I were at an indoor soccer stadium getting ready to play the next game. (For the record, we are not soccer players; we just played on a team once.) We were lacing up our shoes in the stands next to the bright green turf while watching the game. It was a quick play—the ball went from one side to the center, and the player swung his leg back to attempt a goal. He stubbed his toe and snapped his ankle straight back. You could hear the break. Andre and I, sitting side by side, immediately experienced two contrasting responses. My body jerked backward, as if to flee the situation. At the same moment, Andre started running toward the hurt player. She is a physician's assistant and has trained for this type of emergency. We had two very distinct reactions to a problem directly in front of us. Her mentality was to run toward the problem, and I wanted to retreat. Problem solvers have different strengths that need to shine at different moments. Medical problems are not my category. But Andre is a leader in this field and went toward the situation to help bring instant solutions.

If you want to be a problem solver, you have to position yourself to seek out and engage problems where you have the unique ability to create solutions. Most of the time, we all enjoy running away from problems. Problems take time, energy, and hard work. To solve problems, you have to tear back the layers and change the infrastructure of how things work. Problem solving is never easy, but it is important. You will need to train your mind and passions to go toward the things that most of society chooses to neglect. Problem solvers learn to attack what is broken and begin a restorative process of fixing it. We see the opportunity lurking behind the problem. We see how things could be; we don't get paralyzed by the way things currently are.

2. Understand Your Responsibility

When we position ourselves where problems arise, we will quickly find that more problems exist than we can possibly solve. As you start to see more problems, you will be forced to ask questions to evaluate what your involvement can be. Every problem needs an opportunity-evaluation process. That may sound like a big title, but in short, you have to decide what you can do and/or what you need to do for any given situation.

Option 1: No, Thank You. My dad used to say, "I wouldn't touch that with a ten-foot pole." You always have the option to say "No, thank you" to a presented problem. It's okay to not be involved in every problem. If you try to do everything, you will accomplish nothing. Problem solvers understand they can't solve every problem in the world. Be picky, do the things you are designed to do, and cheer on the solutions of others.

Option 2: I'll Connect You. You may feel compassion toward a problem, but you know that your strengths can't match the needed solution. Your responsibility should be to connect that problem with others who can help with solutions. In this situation, you engage by using social capital and networks to introduce the problem to other leaders. This could include personal introductions to the situation or broadcasting the need through your streams of communication. When we become aware of a need, it is often our responsibility to do something with it and help in the resolution, but it may not include our personally solving the problem.

Option 3: I'll Help You. You see a problem, and your abilities can help tackle a portion of that need. Commit to where you can best help. You understand the problem is big. You see that someone is tackling it well; they just need help. You become an adviser, a sounding board, an activist, or a working member of that team. This shows an accurate understanding of who you are and what you do. You dig in because you care and have something to contribute. Too often innovators try to create their own solutions instead of working with other creators to make the project greater. Find your place and attack it.

Option 4: I'll Solve This. This is when a problem confronts you and you can't shake it. You look to make sure that no other person around you can truly bring it the attention it deserves. You have a deep sense of responsibility to lead, give vision, and solve. This is the problem that you find the deepest sense of purpose in pursuing.

3. Be in the Clouds with Feet Touching the Concrete

Idea people are all around us. The people who actually implement their ideas are few and far between. I struggle with solely being a visionary, having my head in the clouds all the time. It is one of my greatest strengths, but it can also be a weakness. If I am dreaming all the time and never get anything done, all I am is an idea guy who never solves a problem.

The other day I heard a business guy say that in order to solve problems, we need 10 percent ideation and 90 percent implementation. Whatever we dream up we need to make happen.

As the leader of a problem-solving initiative, you must always maintain two views. The first view is where you are going: the big picture. You see what others can't see. You see the light at the end of the tunnel. But every day you need to determine the biggest priority to get to that place. Think through steps one to ten—don't jump to number one hundred before it is time. Keep your head up to see and direct where you are going, and make sure your feet are on the ground to determine the next step. Problem solvers need to determine with great clarity what the problem is that they are solving, and they need to know the path toward solutions. Without the path, you are living a dream. Walking the path takes you closer.

Too often people claim to create something new. If it is not a new approach, be honest about it and just work with the people already actively laboring. If you have a viable and sustainable new solution, give it everything you have. You will know it's new and good when people tell you. They will literally say, "That's a good idea." When it's a truly good idea, not just outsiders will applaud your idea; the people who need it most will celebrate your solution. When you have created a viable solution, that solution will endure. When it holds up, needs will be addressed.

At our retreats, we push hard on these issues to be sure the idea people are thinking through implementation. Here are some questions to ask about the problem you are trying to solve and how to begin a process toward a solution:

What is the problem you are trying to solve?

Who is needed to solve the problem?

What makes your solution an innovative and world-shaking approach?

How will you accomplish this solution?

What are others saying about your solution?

What do you need to start today, and what do you need to stop today?

How will the idea sustain itself?

How will you attract other leaders and invite them toward action on this problem?

If you can honestly and thoroughly answer these questions, you are on the path to problem solving.

4. Tell a Memorable Story

Problem solving will never happen alone, but it can be difficult to find collaborative partners. In a society hit with thousands of headlines every day, the challenge of every problem solver is to find a way to tell the story of what is broken in our society in a way that resonates with those who can fix it. We need to learn the art of telling the story. We have to paint what is wrong and cast the vision of how it could be different someday. We need to be winsome in our approach. A picture is still worth a thousand words; the problem is that we see thousands of pictures every day. Casting a unique, memorable, and inspiring vision of a solution is one of the problem solver's critical roles in order to attract others to join in his or her passion.

Compare your story with the best, and challenge yourself to tell the most compelling story possible. Learn from the best because you are competing with the best problem solvers around. Tell the story better than good. We don't realize it, but we are all becoming instant curators of what is good in story creation. We experience such a magnitude of content that if something stands on its own, it must be special.

Mahatma Gandhi once declared, "The difference between what we do and what we are capable of doing would suffice to solve most of the world's problems." I end with the beginning word of our mantra for this chapter. A huge part of social innovation is celebrating that first word: *we*. Bob Goff helped me clarify my own vision by pointing out that "there are many things we can do, but only a few things we are made to do." The beauty in a community of like-minded people is that we have the opportunity to collectively bring solutions to our society.

When I chose to call my organization Plywood People, I had not thought through the literal ramifications. Every week I get an email solicitation from a wood distributor somewhere in China asking me to purchase their product. Of course, we don't sell plywood, and we are not in the industry of purchasing plywood. It's a metaphor. The story behind the name is this: Every time I visit a place in need of restoration, I notice that plywood is present. It is used to fix problems. It is the first step of the solution to a long-term struggle. Additionally, I repeatedly meet some of the most inspiring people in those places. This is why we started calling them plywood people. *Plywood* is a manufactured wood product found everywhere. Plywood layers are glued together so that adjacent plies have their wood grain at right angles to each other. There are usually an odd number of plies so that the sheet is balanced—this reduces warping. Because of the way plywood is bonded, it is very hard to bend it perpendicular to the grain direction. The image of plywood is a visual example of community. Multiple people working together from all directions to solve needs. It makes us all stronger when we work together. As my friend Klayton Korver, cofounder of Seer Outfitters, declared through thousands of T-shirts, "We are better together."

There will be no significant problem that you will ever solve by yourself. It takes many people with unique strengths working together to make a change. As a problem solver, one of the greatest responsibilities you have is to attract other talented people to your solution and retain them over a long period of time.

The first bubble you will have to pop is the hope that all your friends will join you in the pursuit. I think we hope that when we create something, all our closest friends will want to do it with us. But they will not all want to solve the same problem. Your hope will fade quickly. The most unlikely will join you. Prepare yourself now; it doesn't work as you think it will.

We also imagine people who will join us in our pursuit to be from a certain demographic. It will be different from what you have imagined. But this is good. The people you think you need are not the people you truly need. You need people different from you, people who see the world from a different angle. The more diverse your team becomes, the greater chance you have at tackling a problem. Recruit like-minded people who have a similar passion but operate and see the problem differently. It will make your team strong.

Next, most of the people who join you at the beginning will not finish with you. Every project has early adopters; those same people opt out early. Your team will change over time. The people you start with rarely finish with you. You will burn them out. They will be attracted to other problems, and they will run away. That's okay. You are the one responsible for this problem. Every person who joins you will have a time period they serve with you. When the time comes, let them leave freely so they can help others.

Last, attract the best people you can possibly find. Real problems will be difficult to solve. Surround yourself with a team that is pursuing those solutions hardest to tackle. Fear will limit your creation. Make solutions with courageous people willing to go to the darkest places to create the deepest solutions.

I don't have to solve every problem in the world, in our country, or even in my neighborhood. Together we can do more than any one of us can do alone. We can make a significant dent in the needs of our communities. I can celebrate your work, and you can celebrate mine. We can introduce people to each other and to solutions. We can guide friends to their passions. We can connect one another to people who will help in their solutions. We can share best practices. We can critique each other's work. We can do things better. We can do more working together.

TAKE ACTION

If you regularly use social media, take a few moments right now for an observation exercise. Open up whatever social media tool you use, and look at the last month of what you have shared with the people who watch your posts. How many tweets are about you? How many pictures are focused on self? How are you positioning yourself in culture?

How many times do you promote others, encourage others, or share others' successes? Do your posts bring attention to a specific set of problems? Do you bring joy, encouragement, or motivation to others? What is the tone you set when you add your voice to the conversation?

As you begin to see how you are positioning yourself on the Internet, you will probably see a micro-story of how you are positioning yourself in real life. Making a change starts with being intentional about the story you are sharing with the world. What do you want to be known for? How can you begin to share those values through the outlets you use on a regular basis?

QUESTIONS FOR GROUPS

1. What makes a person a problem solver? How is it different from being an idea person or an inspirational person? How is decision making related to problem solving?
2. Do you want to be a problem solver? Why or why not? If you do, what problem(s) are you uniquely designed to help solve? Share with your group what you would like to be known for.
3. Think of a problem you're currently aware of. What is your responsibility toward it? (For example, no, thank you; I'll connect you; I'll help you; I'll solve this.) How do you know this is your role in that situation?

6

DECISION-MAKING STYLES

How Do You Naturally Make Choices?

Truly successful decision making relies on a balance between deliberate and instinctive thinking.
Malcolm Gladwell

My daughter, Jada, was two when she started caring deeply about how she dressed. She has a knack for looking good in her own unique way. I could never pull off her choices of outfits. Her warm chocolate skin and dark curly hair give her an unending array of color choices, and she knows it. She started with layering clothes, not just jackets, but skirts on top of leggings and matching socks accordingly. Next came shoes. By the time she turned three, she had created her own version of "LittleMissMatched"[1] with mismatched shoes—each pair of which matched in Jada's unique way. Every day she would wear mismatched shoes as if they had come in the box that way. Friends started to comment that only she could wear shoes like that.

The same day she wore her favorite outfit (with mismatched shoes) to her school photos, the photographer posted her full-length picture on the website, further confirming her blossoming sense of style. She has a gift of fashion confirmed by photographers—at the age of three.

Like Jada, we all have unique styles. These styles drive not only what we wear but also our approach in solving problems.

WHAT IS MY DECISION-MAKING STYLE?

Psychologists, sociologists, and other scientists continually seek to understand and explain the similarities and differences in people. Many different social, physiological, and psychological factors shape our decision making. There are sociocultural components (external, uncontrollable) and emotional (internal) forces that affect our perception and our decision making. However, most researchers agree that from an early age we begin to see the world through an individualized lens.[2] Though each of us makes up our own combination of ways to think, we also tend to fall into general categories for decision making.

One component is based on our personality and preferred way of thinking. If we like to work a process or prefer to take action, our decision-making style will reflect that tendency.

Another component centers on what we value in life: community, God, luck, risk, predictability, courage, order, process, vision, and so on. For instance, if we value predictability, we will naturally tend toward making decisions that have a long-term chance of success. If we value risk, on the other hand, our decisions lean toward opportunities for adventure or big payoff.

We also may make a decision dependent on whom we value and how it will affect them. Experience level, past successes and failures, as well as confidence levels also play important roles in how we arrive at decisions.

As I've talked with people over the years, it seems that a few general styles emerge as the natural paths by which most people make decisions. As you look at them, most likely one or two styles will jump out at you as your primary ways of decision making, based on your past experiences of making decisions. I will introduce you to friends of mine who embody the particular styles to assist you in understanding each one. I also want to make clear that I don't believe one way is the correct way to make decisions. They are simply different paths to an end goal. Each has its strength and weakness. We will look at both the positives and the challenges of each style to help you as you walk forward on this path to being a decision maker.

Seven different styles describe decision makers: Gut Reaction, List Checking, Story Living, Data Driven, Spiritually Guided, Collective Reasoning, and Passive Undecided. (Or more briefly: Gut, Listed, Story, Data, Spiritual, Collective, and Passive.) If, after reading through the styles, you don't instantly know what your style is, consider taking our free assessment at www.yesornobook.com— it only takes five minutes to complete. Or take the assessment first, and then read the description. I encourage you, however, to read each of the descriptions. You will learn more about yourself and those around you. You may begin to see your team members, coworkers, partners, or spouse in a new light and appreciate the unique contributions they can bring to your decision-making path.

GUT REACTION

Mike leads a venture capital firm that has invested in over a hundred start-ups, and he will tell you he has never read a full business plan before investing in any one of them. He can tell you if he thinks the idea is worth investing in within five minutes of a conversation, based on his experience and the brilliance of the potential.

This style relies both on feeling and on thinking. He doesn't need to know all the details, but he needs to believe in the potential and be assured he can sleep at night. His intuition plays a significant role in what he chooses to invest capital in, whether it's "financial, social, or intellectual capital." When he chooses to get behind a project, something clicks within him that he sees as potential, worth the energy to support. It just makes sense.

If you are like Mike, you are constantly aware of what your gut is communicating. How your gut responds is how you will make decisions. At most decision points a deep sense or feeling consumes your thoughts and drives how to move forward and when. This style consistently asks questions like: What does your heart say? What feels right? Can I sleep tonight given this direction?

Some people do this from a young age and rely on this sense of intuition throughout their lives. Another gut response is based on years of training and knowledge, reaching a level of instinct. An example of this would be doctors who have studied years to be an expert in their field and when an emergency situation arises in the midst of a surgery, they rely on that past training to make an instant reaction. With very little time to process, they trust their intuition to solve a problem in that moment. They have experience and make choices based on that history as well as a feeling about how the future may unfold. A similar example would be professional basketball players who have trained muscles to respond instinctively to situations in real time.

The greatest gift of a Gut Reaction is the ability to make an instant response to a problem in need of an immediate decision. These people don't mind risk and are confident in their abilities. They make decisions and move on with the next challenge at hand. They also tend to simply take failures as a matter of course, something from which to learn, and continue to move forward without wasting away in regret.

Limitations: Many decisions made by a Gut Reaction could have been more thoroughly researched. Some decisions result in hurting other people who were not included in the decision, people who could have added significant value to the decision-making process. Additionally, sometimes Gut Reactions are emotionally charged instead of strategically processed. Emotions can be powerful but misleading. This style tends to have big wins and hard losses.

LIST CHECKING

Courtney loves to make others' dreams come to life. She listens to the end goal and starts to make a list of all that needs to be done to get the team past the finish line. She also writes down everything along the journey. She has lists for the grocery store, lists of restaurants she wants to try, a bucket list of things she wants to do before she dies, and lists of the guys she has dated. She has lists to organize her lists. And she can't go to sleep until her daily list has been completed. Everything needs to be captured so nothing is forgotten or missed.

She is thorough in her approach as she engages a problem. She wants to know every possible option. She weighs the good and the bad to determine the best. If you were to ask her about a major decision she has made in the last ten years, she could probably open a journal and point to the page that explained all the reasoning behind what she chose, both positive and negative.

If you are like Courtney, you lean toward a List Checking approach in decision making. Going through the process of evaluating all the options is most important. This style will consistently make a list of pros and cons of every possible scenario. They will also role-play their decisions to consider what might happen five to ten decisions down the line given this one choice. They may draw out a decision tree of possibilities and hang it on the wall to determine which long-term scenario they like better. They may look at other similar choices made by friends to determine how a decision played out for them and what they can learn from others' choices. It is common for them to seek counsel from many different advisers to hear what they think about all the options—again trying to build the most comprehensive list of pros and cons.

In the end they will look at all the positive and negative things that could happen and make the most reasonable choice to move forward. They prioritize the process and what it takes to get to the end result. By going through the full process, they will walk away with the best choice, knowing as much as possible what positive and negative consequences lie in either choice.

Limitations: Lists never end. The detail of a pros and cons list continues indefinitely, and List Checkers choose to consistently add another option. As the list becomes longer, it makes choices more difficult instead of simpler. List Checkers can get paralyzed by the length of the list and shy away from making a final decision. Once every conceivable option has made the list, they are often dependent on others to help make the choice, since their list may feel overwhelming.

STORY LIVING

Leroy is the leader of a nonprofit organization that seeds people into developing neighborhoods to intentionally serve their neighbors as an act of love. He is the kind of person who is always changing and leaning toward pursuing the unknown. Over the last five years he has adopted two children, launched a coffee shop, inspired a hundred people to ride with him on bikes for 186 miles, taken his family for a month across the United States in an RV that runs on vegetable oil, created a man cave in his backyard, where he hosts Super Bowl parties with three projectors on the sides of his house, produced an environmental initiative for his neighborhood called Green My Hood, and made the largest mural in the city of Atlanta, covering 150 yards. He lives for the story. He looks for the house with the greatest potential so he can change everything about it and tell the story to every person who walks through the front door. He is a doer of unthinkable action.

If you are like Leroy, your decision-making style is Story Living. If you believe that the greatest adventure in life is always the best choice, you are driven by the story. Adventure is king. Story Livers want to catch the biggest fish, climb the highest mountain, and go where no man has gone before. Survival trumps reason. In fact, the most unreasonable option is usually the preferred choice because the most reasonable is too predictable and boring. The only reason to take risk into account is to determine what would be the most courageous option and to prioritize that choice in every situation. YOLO (you only live once) is not just a statement you say to others; it is a core value to this style of decision maker.

Everyone loves a Story Living person sitting by the campfire late into the evening. They own the stories worth telling. If you make choices based on the story, it is rare that you will do the same thing twice. Your choice will commonly lean toward a new experience for the chance of experiencing the unknown.

Limitations: When everything you do is for the story, it is rare to have consistent decisions. Others can look at this style as lacking responsibility or stability. These people live for the next great story, often at the cost of long-term commitments to relationships and employers.

DATA DRIVEN

George is an analyst. He takes numbers, makes sense of what is happening, and can make fairly accurate predictions of what is to come.

His checkbook is up-to-the-minute balanced. One of his greatest frustrations is when he has written a check to a person and that person has not deposited it yet. He understands all the variables of what could happen and plans accordingly, watching the weather for a jacket of choice or when to bring an umbrella.

Time is organized to proactively take the risk of life out of the equation. A structured approach over a long period ought to have predictably successful results. He doesn't just think through a monthly budget, he has five-year projections for his personal life, including a variable for if and when a baby comes into the family, even considering how diapers would impact life three years from now. To any business he is essential, because he sees what others don't see based on trends through research, sales numbers, and cost implications.

If George sounds like you, your decision-making style is Data Driven. This style needs all the information before making a decision. Numbers are the leading indicator for how to proceed. Data Driven people often check the weather forecast daily to decide what to wear. And forecast is not just for the weather; it is the indicator for all decisions. The more information that can be gathered, the better the decision.

Data Driven decision makers often categorize information on a spreadsheet or a series of spreadsheets to quantify them against each other. They may even create a graphic that depicts the future implications for each of the choices. A job offer could be determined simply by the dollar amounts or probabilities of success, failure, or promotion. Documentation of choice will be categorized and ought to be explained to anyone looking for the answer to the question why. Personal research is good, and expert research is better. Long-term planning will always be weighted heavily in their choices. Data will drive decision, and without enough data a decision should not be made.

Limitations: Expectations are not always met. Life doesn't always give the data needed to make a decision. When all the data cannot be found, Data Driven people struggle to make a choice. Outlier situations can alter a plan in an instant by causing a shift in data. Relationships with people who have non–Data Driven styles can cause this style much stress. In short, if the data is inconclusive, these people struggle with decisions.

SPIRITUALLY GUIDED

Ron is the leader of a nonprofit organization and has raised millions of dollars for the ministry over the last fifteen years. He has lived in a Spanish-speaking country for all those years yet has never learned the language. During this time, he has been meeting needs in this community, and the organization has obtained a house in the city to host short-term mission trips, built more than a thousand homes for widows within a one-hour radius of the city, developed a mountain-based camp, drilled a well for clean water for the entire mountain, started a shoe factory, built a home for women affected by the sex industry, and more.

How has all of this happened? Ron would answer: prayer. The first built structure they added to the mountain property was a prayer chapel that overlooks the entire city. Hours upon hours of prayer have made this place come to life. Ron has never sent a direct mail piece for funding; he just prays, and he has been directed. To many rationally guided people, this makes no sense, and neither does his style of decision making. But this is how he is led and makes decisions. In every decision he makes, he seeks simply to be guided by the voice of God, and the results speak for themselves. God has led him to create things far beyond what he ever imagined. Matthew 7:7 is a driver for this style: "Ask and it will be given to you; seek and you will find; knock and the door will be opened to you."

If the approach Ron takes in life resonates with your soul, your decision-making style is Spiritually Guided. Prayer will always trump reason, experience, data, or knowledge. Spiritually Guided decision makers can have all the information that anyone could give them, but they won't make a decision unless they have true clarity from Someone greater than themselves. At times they will separate from others to fast and pray for direction, or they will pursue spiritual disciplines for a period of time as an act of commitment and request for direction. They find decisions through reading the Bible, listening for a spiritual message from a friend or stranger, or waiting for audible direction from God. Decisions will be confirmed through an inner peace and confidence. Sometimes their decisions may not line up with reason, but they gain assurance from a perspective and passion that all things are possible with the help of a greater Being directing their decisions. Making choices in this style will always be spiritual and bring them closer to God in the process.

Limitations: Sometimes Spiritually Guided people hear a direction for their next steps that is not consistent with their experience or giftedness. This can create tensions with those in their community who may not affirm the decision. There are also times when choices seem to be directed spiritually but don't come to fruition. These experiences can discredit Spiritually Guided people's discernment in their communities or cause them and others to question the existence of God. Spiritually Guided people often wrestle with the tension of hearing direction from God and how it lines up or does not line up with confirmation from humans.

COLLECTIVE REASONING

Chris leads a company of over three hundred young leaders partnering with schools to raise funds for their scholastic programs. The reason he does it has nothing to do with the business plan; rather, he has created a business that gives him an opportunity to live out his passion of investing in the next generation and spending time with others. He defines success by the number of people he mentors. The greatest day in his year is any day spent with others. If you were to follow his online stream of pictures, you would notice that 80 percent of the photos are group shots, because he values the collective. He is the gatherer of every party, because if there is no party there is no life. He is naturally inclusive and is always planning the next event. He rallies the troops to create synergy, momentum, and life for the team. Chris is a people person; the more people around him the better.

If Chris sounds like you, your decision-making style is Collective Reasoning. These people make decisions in groups and consider friends their most valuable component in decision making. They tend to believe that if we can all agree on a decision, it will be the best decision for all. They gather groups of people together to talk through all the possibilities and want to make sure they see every angle of choice and all the people it could affect. By having more people in the room, they believe they can make a greater and more informed decision. Jury trials and democratic elections are preferred systems worth believing in and fighting for. They care about people as the priority and will stand up for inclusion and fight against exclusion.

These team builders care deeply about what others think of them. They are synergists and do everything in their power to ensure everyone is getting along. In all cases they will try to make choices that don't alienate individuals but rather make the greatest number of people happy.

Limitations: Many life decisions, while benefiting from community input, ultimately must be chosen by an individual. When you buy a house, you can't have your entire community sign the mortgage. Many choices need to be made by individuals, and very rarely does a group have 100 percent consensus. The worst-case scenario for Collective Reasoners is leading a team that takes a vote with a result divided straight down the middle, with the final decision resting on their shoulders. If all choices are dependent on all people, very few things will get done. Additionally, choice by committee can often be driven by random opinions of the collective that lose sight of a singular vision. Without a leader's vision and direction, a group can lose focus and not move forward to accomplish the vision.

PASSIVE UNDECIDED

Kerry is an accountant who enjoys being behind the scenes and enhancing the lives of others. For her, change happens only when it is forced. She loves people. Disruption of any plans she or others have made is the last possible option. Until just recently, she had never quit a job for fear of how it would affect the business she was working for, even though she knew it was time to move on. Recently, she got a new full-time job but kept doing accounting for her friend's organization because she did not want to mess up their system. She worked late into the evenings and Sundays to try to juggle both. She will never opt out of an email list if she has met the person behind the communication. When friends plan things, she will be there. If she absolutely can't make it, chances are she won't respond. "No" is the hardest word in the dictionary for her. Her joy comes from being a background presence and watching others succeed. She celebrates when others' plans come to life regardless of her involvement.

If Kerry's story sounds familiar, your decision style is Passive— you don't make decisions. This may not seem like a style at first glance, but it is more widely used than we realize. When there is a decision that needs to be made, this style retreats from the tension. They would let anyone else choose what to do for them rather than be forced to make a choice themselves. They truly are fine with whatever happens next, and they are willing to deal with any choice as long as they don't have to make the choice themselves. They believe they can make a decision but prefer not to. In general, they would rather stay out of the fray of large decisions and let the rest of the world determine how to progress. Even when a decision directly influences their lives, they would choose to let whatever happens, happen.

Limitations: If you are Passive, problems are not solved and often you have gifts that are not being utilized. You tend to hope things will work themselves out, but you may be shortchanging those around you of what you have to contribute. Over time, Passive decision making can create dissension in relationships because others will think you don't care about them or are not valuing the friendship. Passive Undecided people struggle with creating boundaries in work and relationships and rarely say no in any situation, even when they know they should.

THE BLENDED DECISION

As you read, you may have identified yourself as a blend of two or three different options. These are not meant to be hard and fast dividers as much as ways to consider the decision-making process and solving problems. I am not advocating one style as right and another as wrong. Each style is unique to who you are and how you feel confident navigating everyday life.

What I have discovered over time is that the wisest choices are often cross-referenced through a few styles. This tends to broaden our perspectives and offer a stronger basis for moving forward in decisions. Later in the book, we will discuss the benefit of gathering people around us who offer us these different perspectives when we are more prone to look at an issue only through our own lenses.

I also think the problem, at times, ought to drive the style you prioritize. The context of your choice should definitely have an influence on your decision-making style. Three contexts that often change your style are the subject matter, the timeline, and your designated role. Mature people can train themselves to make decisions in ways that are not consistent with their normal style so as to best fit the context.

Regarding subject matter, for instance, medical decisions that need to be made in my family easily lead me to be passive. The medical field is my wife's expertise and not mine. Or consider when you are down to the wire and have to make a decision that depends on a narrow timeline. You may be forced to make a gut reaction decision even if you would prefer to gather data. And last, you may prefer to make gut decisions, but as the leader of a task force at work, you must gather the consensus of the entire team if you want their active participation moving forward. In many contexts we can teach ourselves to let our natural style take a backseat to the best style for that moment of choice. The situation at hand may require a much different style of choice than we would naturally pursue.

As you process your unique decision-making style, I recommend talking through it together with your community or team. Not only is it helpful to understand each person's preferred decision-making style, but our team can often help us better understand our own style. We can also work together to encourage each other's decisions and processes and come together to mitigate the potential weaknesses of one style. Understanding how we make decisions helps us understand each other at a core level and helps us encourage each other in different styles. Inviting other styles into your decision-making process will always make your choices better.

THE DECISION-MAKING PROCESS

Now we will walk through a six-step process of decision making. As we proactively become decision makers who are solving problems, I recommend creating a process for decisions. Making decisions based on your style alone limits your problem-solving abilities. If you have the time and want to improve your ability to make good choices, consider a process for getting to answers for your problem.

Not every decision needs this depth of consideration, but there are a handful of decision-making moments every year that ought to go through this process. We will add more insight, questions, and ideas in each chapter, but I want to outline the steps of this process for you along with the decision-making styles that are most useful for each step.

Prayer should be included in every portion of this process. For clarity in your choices, prayer should be a priority not for only the Spiritually Guided style.

1. Explore the Options

We often see a very limited perspective of what could be. It is important to consider what all the possible options may be. Try to include the most unreasonable options in your process, because they could cause you to think of new solutions. Ask a Story Living person in this phase to add to your options, as he or she will come up with extreme ideas that can get you out of the normal box of thinking. Then process the good and the bad of all the options to find the most reasonable few. Ask List Checking people at this stage to help organize your options for future consideration.

2. Understand Who Is Influenced

The people affected are important in every decision. Every major decision we make will cause other people's lives to change in some way. Sometimes they are people very close to us and other times they are very distant in relationship, but other people are always affected by our personal choices. Take time to process what your decision will do to the lives around you, get clarity on what could happen, and consider how that makes you feel. Collective Reasoning people can be assets at this stage as well as the next. They bring the ability to see and value each person in the process.

3. Invite Others to the Table

Once you understand your options and the people this decision affects, it is time to receive feedback from trusted advisers on how to move forward. Just as a Collective Reasoning person would seek counsel, you should as well. Who are the people you can invite to the table to speak into your major decisions? If you are not naturally a Collective Reasoning style, it may be beneficial for you to sit down with someone who is, to ask that person about how to go about soliciting input from others. This can be a learned skill that could multiply your effectiveness exponentially.

4. Name Your Fears

Don't be under the illusion that if you are pursuing your calling you will not be afraid. For some, fear is a constant companion, barking at our heels as we strive to do things no one has done in quite the same way. This is another good time for a Story Living style to speak into your process. These are the people who either know no fear or constantly knock fear over on the way to a great story. Sit and listen to their stories, and steal some of their confidence for yourself.

5. Make Time for Solitude

This is the time to seek spiritual guidance and clarify what you truly believe about the decision. Stop everything to ponder and pray. Separate from others, take all the information you have gathered through this process, and begin to understand what you feel is most important. If this is new to you, sit down ahead of time with someone who is a Spiritually Guided style. Ask them what they do and how they do it.

6. Take a Step Forward

At this point, you have to make a choice. You can't control everything in the future, but you must progress forward toward a decision that feels right to you. Understanding all the knowledge you have gained, it is time to make a decision.

We each have unique styles that drive decisions—they are usually both our strength and our weakness. May we use our collective community, each with different decision-making styles, to help us navigate through our moments of tension. Now let's dig deeper into this process that will help us make the best choices in times of uncertainty.

TAKE ACTION

Just as my daughter, Jada, has a unique fashion style, we each have a unique decision-making style. This does not define us, but it teaches us about others and ourselves. Since the first time I wrote about these decision-making styles, I have been sharing them with people around me and having some lively conversations. Consider who you could talk through these styles with to learn more about one another. Do you have a team that could benefit from this understanding of one another? Take the list, email out the assessment, and gather over a meal for a discussion of your personal styles. Consider these three conversation starters:

> 1. What is your personal decision-making style?
> 2. How have you positively and negatively used your style for decision making in the last three months? Share detailed stories.
> 3. Now that you understand my unique style, how have you seen this play out in my life and my interactions with you?

QUESTIONS FOR GROUPS

1. Begin with the three conversation starters listed above.
2. How have you experienced the strengths of your preferred style? The weaknesses?
3. If you could develop one alternate style more fully, which one would you choose? Why? How can you go about doing that? What help do you need?

THE DECISION-MAKING PROCESS

7

A PILE OF CHIPS

Expand Your Options

*There is no passion to be found playing small—in settling for
a life that is less than the one you are capable of living.*
Nelson Mandela

It was a routine Tuesday at work. I closed my computer at 4:45, walked down the stairs from my office, went outside, and stepped into my car. I did what I always do. Stashed my messenger bag on the floor behind the driver's seat. Put the key in the ignition and dialed Andre from my favorites list on my phone. I always call her to let her know I am on my way home. Her parents were in town, so I knew I needed to be home early for dinner.

She answered the phone quickly to let me know she was at the grocery store to pick up a few things for dinner. We were about to hang up when she added, "Oh, I almost forgot. There's a little surprise for you at home. I can't really explain it over the phone; you just have to see it—okay, bye." It wasn't anywhere near my birthday or Christmas, and she didn't even give me a chance to ask a question before she hung up. Surprises have the potential to make your day, change your day, or hinder your day. She had my attention.

Grateful that my office was only a mile from the house, because curiosity was getting the best of me, I pulled into the driveway behind my in-laws' car. I stepped out, grabbed my bag, and peeked around their SUV to find the surprise waiting for me along the side of our house. It was waiting for me right there in the driveway, in plain sight—you couldn't miss it. The surprise wasn't a car. It wasn't a puppy. And it wasn't a basketball hoop. All of these had crossed my mind on my drive home. I was secretly hoping for that new hoop. Nope, instead my surprise was a pile of wood chips.

Just what I always wanted? The bigger surprise was that this wasn't just any old pile of wood chips. I think I can safely say it was a mountain of wood chips. I'm telling you the truth; I am not making a mountain out of a molehill. This was the biggest pile of wood chips I had ever seen at a personal residence. Being from Michigan, the only thing I can relate it to is the towering pile of snow at the edge of the asphalt after a truck plows a good-sized parking lot.

That pile of chips stood at least ten feet wide, thirty feet long, and ten feet high. There were easily enough wood chips to cover at least four full properties in our neighborhood. One of my first thoughts was, *We don't even own a wheelbarrow.* I had not asked for this wood chip mountain; it had been given to me. Sometimes decisions are made for us. In these moments the questions become,

How will we respond? What will we do with what we have been given?

You may be wondering how this pile of chips appeared in our driveway. I was soon to find out. That morning, Andre and her mom, Sandy, were in conversation about our backyard community garden. The previous year, Atlanta had gone through a severe drought, and harvest was significantly affected by the lack of water. Mulch is one way to assist the soil in retaining water and staying cool, so Andre and Sandy determined that mulch would be a good addition to the garden. Sandy heard that tree-cutting services sometimes gave people their wood chips after they took down a tree. So she and Andre searched online for a local tree-cutting service and hit the jackpot with their first call. The tree cutters were working in the area and had a full truckload of chips ready to drop off that morning. They may have mentioned that a truckload was twenty cubic yards, but Andre only clearly heard "free wood chips," and the rest is Shinabarger family history. Let's just say her style is Story Living, not Data Driven. She said yes as fast as her heart was beating with the excitement over the deal of a lifetime, and two hours later our driveway had more wood chips than a beach has sand.

Fast-forward five hours and I am standing in my driveway with my mouth dropped open, staring at this mound of chips, pondering my options.

Option 1: We could cover the entire yard with wood chips six inches thick, never have to mow grass again, and bury the garden for the ease of an entirely wood chip landscaped property.

Option 2: We could put signs in front of the driveway for free mulch and share it with the community.

Option 3: We could light the pile on fire and hope our house didn't go up in flames with it.

Option 4: We could update our social media streams and offer free wood chips to every person we knew.

Option 5: We could turn it into a play area for neighborhood kids to play King of the Mountain.

Option 6: I could get back into my car, drive back to work, and call Andre to let her know I would not return home until the pile was gone. (This wasn't really an option, but crazy things go through my head at moments like this.)

Option 7: We could rent a dump truck and fill it with the wood chips we didn't need to take to someone who did.

Option 8: We could start bagging the wood chips and place them in every friend's car that came to our house over the course of the entire summer.

Option 9: We could send an email to nonprofit organization leaders and offer them free wood chips for their landscaping if they were willing to come with a truck and pick them up.

Option 10: We could borrow a wheelbarrow and start filling in the garden, postponing further decisions until we saw how much was left.

The options were literally endless. We were given so many wood chips that most of the options listed were implemented at some point that summer. (Of course, I did not drive away and leave Andre, but there were times that summer when I pondered the reality that you never know what you're getting into when you get married.) Every week for the entire summer, from Memorial Day to Labor Day, we spent a minimum of three hours shoveling wood chips and moving them elsewhere. The last wood chip left the driveway after four months of shoveling, pushing, bagging, sharing, and lamenting our sore arms and backs. I may have mentioned to Andre that if I ever saw a pile of wood chips in our driveway again, option 6 was going to happen.

On the upside, that pile of chips caused me to use all my powers of creative option exploring to complete the task at hand. It went beyond a simple yes or no question of whether or not we were keeping the wood chips. A huge pile of wood chips had taken over our driveway, and the only people responsible for moving them were Andre and me. The wood chips taught me that some problems require us to create a greater number of options to get closer to solutions.

OUT OF YOUR MIND

Not every problem is quite as clear-cut as the pile of chips in my driveway. When faced with the task of solving a problem, though, we need to take the time to explore the options. In our increasingly connected and resourced society, the number of options is far more expansive than we can initially conceive. Rather than get stuck following what we think is the only path forward, great problem solvers utilize the opportunity of options as a starting point. Here are some best practices I have learned to increase our options in problem solving.

What Is the Problem?

Before doing anything else, write down the problem as clearly and succinctly as possible. When the problem resides only in your head, it tends to take up more and more space, growing internally beyond its original size. Take a few minutes and get the problem out of your head and onto paper so that it's clear. Then take some time to list the first run-through of options. What can you think of right now that you see as potential solutions to the problem? It doesn't matter at this point how many options you can list. Just start the process of pulling all the random ideas out of your head and making them into concrete form. Number them. Circle chart them. Sketch them in pretty boxes. Use a chalkboard, a whiteboard, or chalk on your clean driveway (if it is cleared of wood chips). Draw in color. Write in pencil. Use colored pencils on white paper or black pens on colored paper. Find a medium that helps you think and get your options out where you can see them.

Expand Your Options

When confronted with a problem, we can quickly jump to the most obvious solution, limiting the possibilities, or we can take time on the front end to broaden the list, imagining new ways forward. We all get stuck at times with situations that on the face of them offer choices we don't like. There may, however, be other options. Before jumping ahead to some foregone conclusion, it's important to step back and look at all the possible options, including some that have potentially never been considered before. As a problem solver, I want to get to a place where I am choosing among an array of innovative options to come up with new solutions to old problems.

To increase our options in moments of choice, we need to challenge our imagination to think in new ways—an expansion of options.

As I work through the option-expansion process, I look at four variables at work in any situation: time, impact, person, and emotion.

The first variable is time. How long do you have until you must make a choice? In our very time-oriented American culture, we tend to subconsciously assume that faster is better. When faced with a choice, especially one presented by someone else, we often feel pressed to make a decision immediately. This is rarely a necessity, especially given that another person's urgency may not fit with your priorities.

Give yourself permission to carefully consider an answer before giving it. And recognize that often time is less of a factor than initially thought. Consider if there is a short-term decision that could be made in order to allow a greater amount of time to think through the longer-term strategy. The first option-expanding strategy is to accurately assess the time constraints for what you are doing and then move forward accordingly.

The second variable is impact. Determine the implications of the decision for your personal life and the team you are leading. How does this decision impact the next thirty days or next five years?

Some decisions require fewer options because they affect very little over the course of time and can quickly be resolved. Other decisions set the course for many years to come, influencing how you live life or do business. These decisions beg for a clear path forward in keeping with the values and vision you espouse. Understanding the short- or long-term implications of a decision will help determine how much energy you should commit to the process. If a decision has a long impact on life, take the needed time to choose wisely.

The third variable is the person. Are you the best person to make this decision, or should another person be guiding this choice? If this choice has personal implications for you and your family, then by all means you need to be involved. On the other hand, if this decision is a team decision that will impact others, make sure you are the best person to make the choice. Some choices are best made not only with the input of others but by sharing the power of choice with the people most invested in the outcome. Is this a one-person decision, or does it need to be a democratic decision?

This is where knowing our own decision-making styles can help us think through a better process. While a Gut Reaction person naturally defaults to individual decision making and a Collective Reasoning person defaults to including everyone, this variable reminds us to use the right process for the right decision. If some other person or people ought to be involved, invite them into the process. If it's not necessary, then take the responsibility to make the choice.

The fourth variable is emotion. Emotion often plays a role in speeding up the timeline. Make sure that the timeline is true to the problem and that your emotions and the emotions of others involved are calm and reasonable before moving forward. When emotions drive decisions, the potential for regret increases. When in a heated decision-making moment, try to stop, gain composure, and consider the possibilities before responding.

Make yourself aware of the physical signs of emotional stress. My eyebrows tend to wrinkle up in those moments. Others may tap their fingers together or close their eyes or feel their body temperatures rise. Lately, when I notice my eyebrows furrowing, I try to stop and force myself to smile. The physical act of smiling shifts my emotions from intensifying the stress to knocking it down a few levels. I have friends who stand with their hands open and palms up in these moments. Many people take three deep breaths. Create a way for you to recognize your emotions, and teach yourself to pause your emotions and reengage your thinking so that you can imagine your options.

PROBLEM-SOLVING OPTION EXPANSION

Once we have established the variables, we can move forward in the fun work of problem solving. In their book *Decisive*, Chip and Dan Heath wrote, "When we widen our options, we give ourselves the luxury of a real choice among distinct alternatives."[1] Taking the time to explore a variety of options pulls us out of survival mode and into the luxury of finding a truly good choice.

A great place to begin the expansion of options is to research the story behind the problem. Begin with the history. What previous decisions led us to this moment of choice? When there is a problem we are trying to solve and a decision that is contingent on that problem, there is often a history that has led us to that moment. Backtrack to understand and have a full scope on how we have made it to this decision point. When we process the full story, it often reveals a deeper problem than the choice currently at hand. Find and fully understand the biggest problem before deciding what is next in a series of decisions.

After understanding the historical context, jump ahead to look at the future. Be sure that you clearly understand and remember the

long-term vision, where you are headed. Consider how this decision will affect your potential future. In the book *Unstuck*, Keith
Yamashita and Sandra Spataro submitted two questions to explore
both the range of choices and potential as well as current limitations: "Given a clean slate, what would we do to live out our vision?
Given the hand we've been dealt, how should we proceed?"[2] These
two questions offer the gift of perspective. One is a visionary expansion question that allows you to think in the clouds. The other is a
tactical question that brings you down to the nitty-gritty of next-step
implications. Both questions are essential, as they keep our brains
creatively engaged in the big picture while moving us forward in
real-world action. When we are paralyzed with indecision, both perspectives offer us ways to move ahead both mentally and physically.

When I think about holding the twofold tension of what is and
what can be, I picture the Krog Street Tunnel in Atlanta. The tunnel
connects two neighborhoods—Inman Park and Cabbagetown—and
is about a hundred yards long. The distinctiveness of the place is the
art collected inside. The length of the tunnel is covered with graffiti. I
have never been to the tunnel and seen the same art twice. Every wall
is full of expression, the graffiti artist's solutions to the world's problems. Some solutions are more graphic and some more inspirational,
but that tunnel reminds me that even in one little tunnel there are
endless possibilities.

I have a photograph of the tunnel framed and hanging next to
my desk to remind me that there may be a different way to look at
the same problem. I can't imagine how many coats of paint are on
those walls, a beautiful collage of thoughts, images, and actions in
one place, turning a dark tunnel into a conversation. Within the

confines of your problem and your context, there are options. Take the opportunity to explore them.

NO. YES, AND. MAYBE.

Ken Robinson defined imagination as "the ability to bring to mind events and ideas that are not present to our senses."[3] To gain more options for the decision at hand, we must engage our imagination with fresh questions. When we are experiencing the intensity of a major decision, the weight tends to crowd out the ability to imagine. We must push our minds to see what others don't see.

Both my wife and I are competitive game players. From our yearly March Madness bracket competition to Settlers of Catan and sports of all kinds, we like to challenge each other with the thrill of the game as a way to enjoy some leisure time together. To help bring down the stress level in difficult decision times, I like to create challenging games to get my blood pumping and my brain moving. Like the time when I knew I had to send out two hundred emails in two days and I told the entire office that I would challenge myself by doing ten push-ups before every ten emails I wrote. I needed to get pumped up. The entire office was cheering me on as I pushed my way through those two hundred emails.

To create new possibilities, I need to look at problems in a different way. One of my brain games is called No. Yes, And. Maybe.

1. Say No to the Current Solutions[4]
Pretend whatever solutions you currently have on the table are not options anymore. Say no to all of them for a moment to

force the imagination of new solutions. If you were to say no to all the options you were currently considering, what would you do then? If you were in a completely different situation with the same problem, what might the solutions look like? Take out the constraints of budgets, timelines, and people. What if the current budget were gone? What if money were no object? What if you had to do something right now rather than next month? What if you had two years? What if you had no team? What if you had any team you could pick? Dream bigger. Risk broader. Consider the impossible. Actually imagine the problem being solved. What would it take to get there? How might it happen? Who would you need to attract to help solve the problem? What would be the best choice given the reality that things could actually change for the better?

2. Say Yes, And

Consider the most extreme examples of solutions, the outliers. What could be possible? Then play a game of Yes, And. Start with one simple idea, and instead of ruling the solution out quickly because of its ridiculousness, instinctively say the words "Yes, and" and add to that idea. While this results in ridiculous options that may never be possible, it also shines a bright light on the problem and opens the circle wider to new possibilities you never would have imagined, much less considered. If you say yes to an option, what would you do next and how could you add on to that decision to keep the options continuing? Keep the ideas rolling into one another. Don't stop this process earlier than needed to find a solution.

3. Say Maybe

Maybe you can learn from another problem, solution, or decision. Look around for parallel problems. Our emotions trick us into feeling that no other person has been sitting in our shoes, pondering the same question or dilemma we are dealing with at this moment. No one understands, so no one can help us find the way. It's likely that the detailed elements of our situations are rarely replicated, but we can usually find similar situations with different details.

This parallel concept was first introduced to me by Jennifer Leonard, a creative leader for IDEO and coauthor of *Massive Change*, who uses this in conceptualizing new creative solutions for some of the world's top brands. She looks for parallel industries that came up with new solutions to problems that may be relatable to her clients. Our solutions may not be the same, the details may not be the same, but their innovative ideas may spark the ideas for new solutions in our context. This is one of the primary reasons I am always reading and talking to others. In our unique situations, we still have similar problems. As we study or listen to how others work through their scenarios, we can learn and apply some of their solutions or processes in our own situations. Play the Maybe game: maybe this parallel problem shines light on our own dilemma.

NARROW YOUR OPTIONS

You should now have a comprehensive and imaginative collection of options at this point. Now transition your thinking toward the selection process. Choose the three options you think are the best given all the directions that are possible. Our goal in the options phase is to get to a place where you as the decision maker are choosing from multiple reasonable options. This is not always possible, but more often than not the process should glean for you a series of viable, good, and promising options. From these curated selections, we can start to filter the possibilities through the next phase in the process.

Once you have three good options, consider what might happen in each of the choices to see if you are comfortable with each of the outcomes. Your decision-making style will play a strong role at this point in the process. Use it with confidence. One of the most important outcomes of a strong decision-making process is a sense of confidence within the decision maker. Knowing you have worked a process and knowing how and why you have arrived at a solution assure you that you are doing the best with what you have as you walk forward. Prioritize your options.

THE MIGHTY JUNGLE

It started with a three-hour truck ride. I was in the back of the Land Cruiser with my friend Trey in a "seat" with a three-inch-wide bar across the middle. We were in the jungle in northern Rwanda. They call Rwanda the Land of a Thousand Hills, and it felt like we were going up and down every single one of them. My wife and I, Trey, and about fifteen other friends were bouncing precariously along the road toward an experience of a lifetime.

We arrived and were split into two groups, each led by a guide. Before we left on foot, we were given some strict cultural training. Never make eye contact. If a face turns toward you, look down. If anyone gets close, squat down and look away. We are their guests, visiting their habitat. Off we went following the guide carrying the largest machine gun I had ever seen, loaded with ammunition. Bringing up the rear was a guard with the same type of gun ready to fire at will. We walked for just over an hour in silence through the thick jungle underbrush, our guide carving the way with a machete. Suddenly, we arrived. There right before my eyes were *gorillas*. Silverback gorillas. The guide indicated that they were in a good mood with the leaders of the family asleep. We were given permission to snap some up-close pictures of the two leaning back against a bush snoring away. The eight-member family included two newborns. A wonder to behold. Then they woke up and started playing. The babies swung from the branches and a couple of others batted their chests as acts of courage. A playful family of gorillas wrestling and enjoying one another surrounded us as we watched in awe. We were in their home. It was amazing. Then came the moment I will never forget.

One of the larger gorillas came toward me and looked at me. Of course I immediately looked away and squatted in submission. He wanted to play with me, so he grabbed my shirt and started to pull me with him. Nobody had given me training on what to do when a gorilla decides that I should be his playmate. I had no idea what to do. Do I play? Do I push away? Every muscle in my body tensed in terror. I was stunned. He grabbed my shirt right by my shoulder and pulled hard, dragging me out of the spot where I had been frozen in place. The only option I had at that moment was to let a three-hundred-pound gorilla pull me into his jungle. I unwillingly said yes because you can't say no to a silverback gorilla.

Almost immediately, I felt a foot kick me in the back. It was the trusted guide pulling me away from the gorilla, who lost his grip on me and continued on his merry way. My eyes were as big as golf balls. I looked directly at the four other people in our group who had witnessed the entire thing. Four mouths hanging wide open as stunned as I was. I turned to them and whispered, "I think I just peed my pants." We all laughed with relief, overwhelmed with what had just occurred. I'm pretty sure it took several days for my lungs to breathe normally again. Not only will I never look at a gorilla the same way again, but also my respect level for the species expands far beyond just squatting in submission.

In some moments we have more options than others. We all hope for control as decision makers, but we don't always have it. We wish for more time for choices, but we don't always receive it. We desperately want to know the future, but we rarely can predict it. Some choices lie squarely in the palms of our hands, and at other times we are at the mercy of other decision makers. Sometimes the options can be narrowed to just yes or no, and other times the number of options is limited only by the creativity of our God-breathed souls. Much of the joy of life can be found when we realize what a great privilege it is to live intentionally making choices, remembering all that God has given.

When I read Choose Your Own Adventure books as a boy, I had a routine. When I got to a choice page listing two or three page numbers depending on which route I chose, I would keep my finger in that page as I read ahead. If I didn't like the outcome of the first choice, I would turn back to the original page and find out which page number directed me to the alternate ending. I was constantly balancing choices, not fully moving ahead. Of course, this got tricky once I tried holding multiple choices back while moving forward again and again. I would hold on to a major choice, second-guessing the direction of moving forward. I only had so many fingers, so this practice wouldn't work for very long. Eventually I just had to make a selection and turn the page, letting the chips fall where they may. I was given options and was forced to choose, because as the pages turned, I would need to make yet another choice.

Options will be available at every turn you make in your journey of life. Every decision will open up new opportunities unforeseen at the previous point. Every opportunity creates new challenges to conquer. We are created with the power to choose. We have been given the abilities and knowledge to make wise choices. Given all the options at hand, you have the ability to choose your next adventure. In the next chapter we will be reminded to think of the next step in the process: who will be affected.

TAKE ACTION

To give you a new view of the quantity of options in your daily life, try to track them for one day. This is a very difficult experiment to work through, but it will give you perspective on the amount of choices you are making daily and the amount of options you have per choice.

Let me play this out for you. Your alarm starts ringing, and you have two choices: Do I hit snooze or wake up? Two options. Wake up. Do I get in the shower, start coffee, check my phone for messages, or watch the morning news? Four more options. Watch the morning news. Do I watch *SportsCenter*, *Today*, or *Good Morning*

America? Three more options. Get the idea? In this scenario, before you ever drink coffee in the morning, you have already processed nine options.

This exercise challenges you to see the huge number of options you have even in your everyday life. When it comes to decisions of greater importance, you will have trained yourself to see the assortment of options possible in any given scenario. Expansion of your bank of options will result in better decisions.

QUESTIONS FOR GROUPS

1. How easy is it for you to imagine options beyond the first one or two that come to you? If this is hard for you, what do you think gets in the way? For instance, are you in a hurry to decide because lack of closure feels uncomfortable?

2. What could help you think of more options? For example, do you know someone who could be a sounding board and idea generator? Does writing down your options help you think? What method of writing or drawing would be most helpful? Would researching the history of the problem help? What about reflecting on the variables? What about saying No, or Maybe?

3. Choose a problem as a group. Play with Yes, And—one person proposes an option as a solution, and the next person adds to it by saying, "Yes, and …" Then the next person adds to that with another "Yes, and …" See how far you can get, even if the solutions become outrageous.

8

PEOPLE MATTER

Understand Who Is Influenced

*A community is the mental and spiritual condition of
knowing that the place is shared, and that the people who
share the place define and limit the possibilities of each other's
lives. It is the knowledge that people have of each other,
their concern for each other, their trust in each other, the
freedom with which they come and go among themselves.*

Wendell Berry

I was in the Dominican Republic observing firsthand the power of
microfinance when I also learned the power of saying no. Thirty of us
had traveled across the island for three days, interacting with people
who were lifting themselves out of poverty by taking small loans to
start their first businesses. The thrill of opportunity for all people had
filled me with hope throughout the trip.

One man in particular started a business that still astounds me. He collected empty glass bottles of Coca-Cola and filled them with gasoline. Setting up beside a well-traveled road, he created a makeshift gas station. A motorcycle could stop quickly and fill up with a Coke bottle of gasoline for a dollar. The business owner lined up row upon row of bottles in old waffle-shaped crates one on top of another. As none of the bottles had caps any longer, the smell itself left an impression even from quite a distance away. While the environmental working conditions were not particularly healthy, the innovation and determination to change his life left me feeling intoxicated in all the best ways.

Why is it that at the moments I am experiencing the greatest sense of purpose, I also experience the greatest tensions in decision making? It often seems that just when my world feels right, my outlook hopeful and my actions intentional, I am rudely confronted with a reality check of all that is wrong in the world.

After three days flying high on inspiration and potential from so many Dominican entrepreneurs, the dark side of the island reared its ugly head. Our group convened at a beach resort to debrief and glean more wisdom from leaders who had joined us for this trip. It was our afternoon free time, and people were playing beach volleyball or taking naps on towels by the water. I noticed several small vendors just down the beach and decided to browse for souvenirs to take home to my wife and friends.

The tents were filled with take-home trinkets, from colorful woven blankets to Cuban cigars, handmade purses to hammocks. They had everything you could imagine to entice you to buy a token to remember this amazing place. The tents were basically blue tarps pulled tight and strapped to metal poles about seven feet off the ground. The sun shined so brightly that every place in sight was covered with this blue-toned sun. Under the tents were short tables stacked from sand to tarp, filled with endless products at great prices.

As various items caught my eye, I asked the young, attractive woman in the tent, "How much?" In English, she rattled off prices. By the looks of the whole setup, it seemed that her business was doing well.

Suddenly, she asked me a question: "Do you like massages?" After I gave her what I'm sure was a bewildered look, she got straight to the point. "I give good massages. Full body massages." Wow. Not what I was looking for, so I quickly sputtered out something about just getting souvenirs for my wife.

Not to be deterred, she continued, "I give really good massages. Do you want me to give you a massage?"

"No, I'm okay."

She got closer to me. She was within three inches of my chest. Almost touching me, her face turned quickly from an innocent girl selling souvenirs to a woman looking for something different. "I give *full* body massage."

It was the first time I had come face-to-face with a woman offering herself to me for money, for forty dollars to be exact. There was not a single person around us. I felt blindsided, trapped in a blue tent seeking a new hammock for my back porch with a woman proffering sex for money. I kindly declined.

She quickly came back, "Thirty dollars."

"No."

"Twenty dollars?"

"*No*, thank you."

"Five dollars?"

"*No. No. No.*" I finally pushed her away and ran out of that suffocating blue tent. I ran off the beach. Ran past the volleyball game. Ran directly to my room. My running quickly turned into sobbing.

She had offered herself to me for five dollars.

I had said no.

Once I had pulled myself together enough to talk about it, I sat with a few friends trying to put words to what had just happened. Saying I was distraught is an understatement. I did not have a category to put it in. Inside me was a mash-up of the battle of temptation and self-control, the profound sadness of injustice, and the painful truth that I still lived in a broken world desperately in need of hope.

In a twenty-four-hour period, I had drunk deeply of the hope of entrepreneurialism lifting people out of poverty with dignity and pushed away a proffered cup filled with the dark liquid of exploitation.

Slavery and exploitation are two of the hottest social issues of our day. I have seen movies about the injustice of sexual exploitation and contributed money to combat the issue. Some of my close friends work as far away as Cambodia, rescuing girls from the sex trade, and as close as my home city of Atlanta, running restorative homes for those attempting to escape this trap. I have given of my own strategic time, energy, and influence combating this issue and raising awareness with platforms given to me. But there is no video I have ever watched or story a friend has ever told me that holds a candle to my experience that day.

How could we live in a world that makes a beautiful girl believe she has a body worth only five dollars?

The only real answer at that moment was no. But it is a no that I pray I can turn into a Yes by continuing to look for ways to push back the darkness and hold up the light of hope in our world. I pray earnestly for God to give me eyes that don't see what I can get from a girl like this but instead see what this girl could contribute to our communities. May I see what could be, not only the problem in front of me.

This moment of tension also shows just how directly our decisions influence others. If in a moment of weakness I had said yes, I would have been another person to take a piece of innocence away from that girl—without even knowing her name. If I had said yes, my wife and our marriage would have been forever changed. If I had said yes, I would have contributed money to the industry that so many of my friends have dedicated their lives to end. If I had said yes, I would have chiseled off a piece of my integrity, that deepest part of me that strives to maintain consistency between what I believe and say and do. I would have radically undermined so many of the relationships I have worked so hard to build.

My decisions never affect just me. When I say yes or no, I always impact others.

When I was younger, I truly believed that my decisions shaped only my life, but the older I get, the more deeply I understand how my decisions often influence other lives even more than my own. Major decisions I make have the potential to directly impact three groups of people: my family, my sphere of influence, and my world.

Our choices are not a tack pushed into a spot that makes a tiny hole and stays put. They are more like a rock hurled into the ocean: the initial impact makes a splash, but the waves continue circling out even beyond our ability to see them. Our choices change the lives of others.

When the larger decisions rise before us, it's very important to understand who will be affected by our choices. We usually quickly think about the options but overlook who will be changed and how our choices will shape their lives. Knowing who is affected and in what way can sometimes make a decision for you. Making decisions independent of people offers only a limited perspective at best and is inhumane at worst. Dale Partridge, the founder of Sevenly, and his team have coined a phrase that sums it up well: People Matter.

FAMILY CHOICES

My friend noticed a hole in the street in front of his house. He was waiting on the city to patch the street, but in the meantime, there was this hole about four feet in diameter. One day, my friend and I looked down into the hole to discover a bewildering array of pipes.

Bob Goff taught me that there are many "pipes" of people under my skin, but there is one pipe that supersedes and is larger than all the others: family. When we lose focus on which pipe ought to receive the greatest priority, everything falls out of place. As a husband and father, I make decisions every day that affect my wife and two children. My personal choices of character, priorities, and calling directly affect my family's future. I make numerous choices every day that determine who is most important in my life. The greatest tensions in my life seem to consistently fall in the space between my family and my work.

Here is my disclaimer: I love to remember the moments when I have succeeded in prioritizing my family; unfortunately, it feels like I have more memories of my failures. I am still a young dad and will continue to make positive and negative choices that will shape their lives. On a daily basis, my selfishness or ignorance makes choices that negatively shape my family, but I also daily make strong choices that match my heart and my actions. I want to prioritize my family more every day.

One way I can ensure that I will make more decisions in line with my desires is to stop and create a set of values that help me make decisions. Holding a decision up next to an overarching series of decision-making premises often simplifies choices. The priorities and values you and your family have will be different from those of even your closest friends. What's important is to find your values. Here are a few values Andre and I have agreed upon as a framework for how we make family decisions. Even if you don't currently have a family, they will give you a glimpse of what a set of values might look like in your life.

1. Communicate and Adjust Expectations

The moment comes in the lives of most husbands, fairly early on in marriage, when they realize they have not married their moms. While this may seem obvious for some of you, the rest of us may be a little slower. The only marriage most of us have seen up close and personal is our parents'. Without realizing it, we use this to form nearly unconscious expectations of what roles and responsibilities a wife or husband ought to perform. Couple that with the romantic notion of two people "made" for each other, and the expectations grow to epic proportions.

Best marriage advice: Prepare to adjust your expectations. Your wife will not do the same things your mom did. She is a completely different person with a whole new and wonderful set of strengths and abilities. And the fact of the matter is that marriage is two imperfect people coming together. One of the false ideas of the "made" for each other premise is that somehow our individual strengths will complete one another, magically forming one perfect marriage. I do believe Andre has made me a greater person, and I think she would say the same about me, but it has not come easily. Two imperfect people coming together do not make things more perfect; they make things more complicated. Our individual imperfections become amplified and cause countless moments of tension.

I believe one of the primary problems in marriage is uncommunicated and/or unmet expectations. We expect our partners to make decisions that will benefit us. We are forever disappointed when (gasp!) they are as selfish as we are.

We expect that something that happened without discussion in our growing-up families will automatically happen in our new families. We are horrified when our partners don't seem to know the drill.

We expect that our partners will anticipate our needs and desires at the end of a long workday. We are disillusioned when they choose to meet their own needs in their own way at the end of their equally long workday.

The only way to tackle this problem is to communicate expectations and adjust them. It is not enough simply to communicate an expectation and assume that the other person will naturally live up to it. Expectations often need to be thrown out, or at the very least they need to be adjusted to take into account individual abilities, needs, desires, and preferences. This is the work of two imperfect people choosing to make a new life together.

2. If I Change the World and Lose My Family, I Fail

Over the last two years, I have worked with over eighty social enterprises in the Atlanta area, advising on business planning and sustainability. These people are giving their lives to helping others. The number one tension I hear from these leaders has nothing to do with the strategy, finances, passion, or teamwork within the organization. The number one tension is balancing work and life. Once you commit to doing something that has not been done before, it is easy to give all your time, money, and energy to that project. This leads to a sacrifice greater than anticipated. Often it is your family and close friends who get left behind. Working harder and longer starts to consume entrepreneurs, occupying the mental top shelf at all times.

As I have thought about this work/life issue, I have had a difficult time finding a historical example of a person who succeeded both in changing the world and in raising a family. This lack of balanced heroes has caused me to think long and hard about whether it is possible both to make a huge societal difference in my lifetime and to be a dedicated and involved parent and partner. I still don't have an answer to that question.

My wife and I have determined together that if we have to make a choice, we will choose to raise children who are world changers.

We will not sacrifice our family for anything else. We know it is a commitment that must be made at the front end because the needs and excitement all around us will constantly force us in another direction.

One indication that you may be choosing work above family is if every conversation with every group of people (including your partner) centers on what you are doing and how you are achieving it. If this happens, be concerned. You have lost touch with the needs of others and are starting to find fulfillment in your own self-interest. Don't lose the pulse of the people who matter most to you, or they will be gone. If your family is important to you, make time for them, prioritize them. You may not realize it, but they are the people who usually give you energy to keep going, and you need them. Make a conscious decision to make others more important than your project. Don't get married to your solution. Instead, stay committed to your partner.

3. Busy Seasons End Only by Choice

There is always more work to be done. Don't just read that and move on. Stop and think about the truth of it for a minute. In any worthwhile endeavor, there is always more work than any one person can ever accomplish in a finite amount of time. I used to think that the more hours I worked, the more successful I would become. The problem lies in determining how many hours are enough. It starts with just a few hours, then just a few more hours, and then a whole lot of hours. Don't think that if you just work a few additional hours it will change the trajectory of your work. It won't. Work hard while you are at work, and then go home and be home.

One thing that helps my family is to look forward three to six months and plan a stopping time. Since much of my work is project or event driven, this works well for us. When I know an event is coming up that will take a lot of my time and energy, we plan a vacation or time away immediately after. We regularly do this. It keeps our spirits up, knowing a break and significant family time is coming. A plan also assures my family that I am planning for them. They are just as important as my events, and they get their share of me too.

If you don't take scheduled time away with those you love, busy seasons will run into busy seasons, and you will just be living a busy life. Demands on decision makers are infinite, but your time is finite. Plan to stop.

4. Fear Is Not an Option

We love adventure. We want to be people of courage who raise children of courage. We want our children to understand the world is broken and God has called us to restore this place, relying on Him who is greater than us for their safety and security. Fear creates limits. Fear limits opportunities by stopping us before we even start. Fears are usually rooted in things like money, control, and limitations.

It's easy to get in a rut of making decisions based on staying safe or comfortable. I am always surprised by how many families we meet who have chosen safety as their number one priority in raising children. Instead of living intentionally, families choose schools, neighborhoods, and playgrounds based on which option will have the greatest safety. It's also easy as a family to build a life around financial dependency rather than on goals you truly want to achieve.

Many of us become tied to choices based on those financial fears, which then drive all other decisions. Dreams are rooted in courage and have the potential of adventure, possibility, and life. Dreams can be scary, but they also make life interesting and fun. Andre and I have chosen to say yes to courage and no to fears. Fear will not make decisions for our family.

5. Community Completes Us

Over the years, Andre and I have had amazing communities of people surrounding us. When we are not intimately connected to a community, we struggle deeply. A funny thing we have noticed, though, is that we all think that when times are tough we need to step back and focus on ourselves. Andre and I don't believe this is true. The only way to make it through tough times is with others. We need each other to see our problems, walk through our tensions, and contribute to the solutions.

Andre and I have seen this in community numerous times. When couples start retreating from our community, we know they are having relationship problems. We have had these same temptations. We feel that when we are having difficulties we need to limit the time we spend with others and refocus on ourselves. Most often the opposite is true. Those closest to you often have the insight to see what the two of you cannot. When you take away these loving and wise voices, you can miss what you most need to hear.

The reverse is true as well. If you see people you care about retreating, engage them. They need you. They need your care, your listening ear, and your perspective to help them through whatever has them stuck. We were made for each other. Don't abandon that gift when you or someone else most needs it.

LEADERSHIP CHOICES

I knew something was up. One of my top employees asked to have breakfast with me. We met at a small café, with everyone around us enjoying their eggs and bacon. I had just returned from vacation, ready to dig in to work. She had not. In my absence, she had become more and more overwhelmed.

She had written me a five-page letter that she wanted me to read. It was the only way she knew to get all of her thoughts out in a complete format. The letter communicated everything you don't want to hear about your leadership, and the worst part was that it was all true. She was ready to quit and move on. All I could say to her was that she was right. Everything she had written to me was right. The decisions I was making for the organization were not sustainable, and the person they were most affecting was not me, but her. Every new project, every new idea, every yes amounted to more and more work on her shoulders. In that moment, I understood that the leadership decisions I was making were directly impacting my team in a negative way. I was failing as a leader.

So that's what I told her. I chose to change, and she stayed. Did change happen instantly? No, but learning how my decisions affected others made a significant impact on my choices. At the forefront of my mind now is the battle between my visionary ambitions and the capacity of my team. Once I ask others to join me in this work, my decisions take on a new dimension: the daily lives of others. When I make a decision to change something as I lead people, that simply means that I am changing the lives of my team as well. Every decision a leader makes directly affects someone else. Decisions must be calculated with other people in mind, or before long you will be a person meandering alone instead of a decision maker with influence over a team.

As an innovator, I thrive on creating new ideas. Trying to sustain a team of implementers who can successfully navigate my ideas is one of my greatest challenges. While they are busy making one of my previous new ideas work, I am off thinking up a new way to do something. I prefer not to take the easy road but would rather do something unique. While different is usually better in my mind, it most often means more work for others.

One of the key people in my work life regularly responds to my newest ideas with a sarcastic "Great idea; now let me just press a button and make that happen for you." Idea people need trusted team members to remind us that every idea requires lots of work to make it happen. There is a fine line between creating results by looking ahead and understanding the speed and pacing of the people who are following us. If we make too many drastic decisions too fast, we alienate our team and make it difficult, if not impossible, to follow. Not all good ideas need to be implemented at the moment of conception. In the words of Scott Belsky, "We are humans, not machines. With our creativity comes the tendency to think of random ideas and actions we might want to take but not right at that time. Idea generation is often tangential to the active projects in our lives. But the fact that the timing is off does not mean that the thought isn't worthy of future consideration."[1] Idea people always have ideas. However, sometimes our good ideas are not good ideas right now.

One beautiful fall afternoon, I was talking with two of the most influential photographers in the Southeast who expressed an interest in doing a unique event. It would be a first-time collaboration for the two of them with the purpose of serving a group of people I cared deeply about. If I were to pay for their time on my own, it would easily have been fifteen to twenty thousand dollars. Instead, they came up with an idea called Help Portrait to provide photo shoots and family portraits free of charge. They wanted to donate their time and expertise to give photos to people who had been displaced due to war or conflict. Overwhelmed by their generosity, and knowing the potential beauty that would result, I quickly agreed to put their plan into action in three weeks. As if the timetable were not already difficult, I also scheduled it to occur the Sunday after Thanksgiving. Of course, this landed after an already grueling fall schedule of events for our team. We pulled it off, but it was not pretty, and my team was exhausted.

My choices affect my team. The idea was phenomenal. The motive was commendable. But the timing and decision-making process negatively affected my team. Every good endeavor is not the best for the people you lead.

One of the most difficult dilemmas is determining when to push ahead and when to slow down. Some decisions have to be made even though they lean more toward the good of the vision than the good of the team. This is the weight of influence. Making decisions that others won't like leads to internal tension. This tension is multiplied when we know that every decision and its consequences will be analyzed by the entire team. This is what decision makers do; we make the hard call. Sometimes we call it right. Sometimes we don't.

As I have lived both realities, I have learned that the one thing I can do is take some time to think it through before making a decision. Four questions assist me in thinking through the ramifications for my team. They don't guarantee a right decision, but they do assist me in being more thoughtful about the needs of those I care deeply about and who have taken the risk to follow me. These questions are:

1. Who Will Be Influenced by This Choice?

Your choice will change lives. Remembering this fact is a critical starting point to making decisions that care for others. Who will feel the effects of this decision? Your decision will change people in both positive directions and negative directions. Take time to write down their names. This takes the decision out of simply an analytical framework and into a humane one. Too often we try to make decisions that are not personal, but more often than not the decisions are personal. Choose wisely, knowing that real people experience the results.

2. How Will This Decision Change Them?

After you pinpoint the people influenced personally by your decision, imagine how this choice will change their lives. Though we are not fortune-tellers, a number of results can be predicted. The actual future is unknown, but based on past experience and knowledge of the situation, we can often anticipate likely scenarios. Take the time to write out a variety of possible scenarios in order to help you think through the positives and negatives of a given decision.

The more prepared we are for the waves of influence, the greater respect and trust others will have in our leadership over time. Use your idea-creating ability to imagine scenarios and solutions, thereby proactively preparing you and your team for the results.

3. What Is the Best Route to Communicate Your Decision?

When you are the decision maker, you have the responsibility to communicate your choices to others directly. I have had to work hardest at this step. Time after time I have disappointed people by my lack of clear communication. Though I have anticipated how my decisions will affect others, I have neglected to take the time to communicate what is coming. Before and after, the decision maker's job is to choose the best way to send the message and then send it. In celebration and in defeat, leaders are the people who share the news. Let them hear it from you. Have the hard conversation. Make a big deal about a celebration. Make a moment memorable and shape how you communicate to others. Clear, honest communication expands influence.

4. What Did You Learn about the People and This Choice?

After you have communicated a decision to your team, take time to separate yourself from others to ponder what you have learned. Every choice that affects others gives you a deeper glimpse into their stories. You will learn things about others that you did not know previously. Process and store that information to assist you in future decisions. When you as a leader make a choice that is filled with tension, you learn critical information about how you lead and what you value.

AFFECTING THE BROADER WORLD

For the last three years, I have been competing for business against China. I lead a project in a community called Clarkston that has been described by *Time* magazine as the most diverse square mile in the entire United States. This community is filled with families who have been displaced from their homes due to conflict, religious persecution, or national disaster. The people of this community have lived nomadic lives for years, and the government refers to them as refugees. Our team consists of refugee women from Burma, Iraq, and Afghanistan. We have a job-training program for these women. We make bags from old billboard materials and coffee burlap bags. We sell these bags often in bulk to large events and brands.

Our biggest competition is a one-dollar reusable shopping bag made in China. Our product is priced higher because we pay fair wages; our competition does not pay wages that are even possible to live on. I understand that budgets drive many of our decisions, but if we make choices that ignore the people we don't know, we are choosing lives of selfish consumption.

The hardest people to consider are the people I don't know, the people I never see. But every day I make decisions that impact their lives. We have all bought products for a low cost and rarely think about how that price affects others. I often make self-seeking decisions; but if we win at the cost of others' humanity, we lose.

Many people have a philosophy that says if we don't see it, it doesn't happen. But it does happen. We contribute to the downfall of others every day with the choices we make. Let us make a difference by considering those affected by our decisions.

DECISION MAKERS THINK ABOUT PEOPLE

When we make decisions, we impact real people. The people can be as close to us as our spouse and kids or as far away as the other side of the world. Crafting an understanding of how our choices shape the lives of others is important. As you make more and more decisions, the quantity of people you influence will probably rise. In each and every collective of people, a few in the group will rise to be the decision makers. Some people call them leaders, some call them influential, but ultimately they have been given the power of choice. Decision makers choose wisely, knowing the implications of what will happen to others both positively and negatively. People matter, and wise decision makers deeply consider other people.

TAKE ACTION

When was the last time you proactively chose a decision that positively shaped the lives of others? Take action. Begin with a box of ten thank-you cards. Think about ten people whom your choices consistently affect. They could include your spouse, friends, team, kids, coworkers, or others. Take time to write each person a note. Make a decision to proactively influence others with positive notes. Think about ways your decisions have affected them in the last year.

Say you're sorry for your mistakes, and share how you hope to play a positive role in the year ahead.

QUESTIONS FOR GROUPS

1. What do you think about this statement: "If I change the world and lose my family, I fail"? Why is it true or not true, in your view? How, if at all, should it affect your decisions?
2. What do you think about this statement: "Busy seasons end only by choice"? Why is it true or not true, in your view? How, if at all, should it affect your decisions?
3. What are some ways your choices affect others? Who are those others? How does understanding this influence your choices?

9

WELCOME TO THE TABLE

Invite Others to Advise You

> *When we honestly ask ourselves which person in*
> *our lives means the most to us, we often find that it*
> *is those who, instead of giving advice, solutions, or*
> *cures, have chosen rather to share our pain and touch*
> *our wounds with a warm and tender hand.*
>
> Henri Nouwen

My elementary school had one of those classrooms with bathrooms in the back of the room, one for boys and one for girls. For twenty minutes I had been in that little closed-door room going number two (as we would say during that era of our lives). I guess I got lost in the moment—with a song stuck in my head. Lollipop, lollipop, oh lolli lolli lolli lollipop. Ba dum dum dum. That catchy tune played through my head over and over again.

The longer I sat, the more comfortable I became. The song started in my head, then moved to a little hum. Before long the hum formed words and I started to sing it out loud. Louder and louder again. Apparently, the acoustics in that tiny room went beyond those four walls. What I thought was a concert for one was instead loud enough for the entire class to hear. I washed my hands and walked out to a standing ovation of sorts.

Everyone was looking at me. The room burst into outrageous laughter, and every kid was pointing at me. In Mrs. Vienna's second grade class at Fairview Elementary School, I realized for the first time that I cared what other people thought of me.

A point occurs in every person's life when you begin to hear the voices around you and realize they are talking about you. Contrary to the popular ditty, those voices and their words hurt just as much as sticks and stones. Yet those same voices also hold strengthening and healing powers beyond what we first imagined. Caring to hear what others say can be good, but discerning which voices to listen to is a make it or break it decision. We all need voices that ultimately believe in us and our abilities.

Three different types of people have the ability to speak into our lives: No People, Yes People, and Advisers. The No People look negatively at every situation. It doesn't matter what you're doing, they will find a way to criticize your work, decisions, and lifestyle. These people rarely make things for the world; they just try to bring down the contributing people around them in order to make themselves feel better.

The Yes People are the ones who will always agree with everything you say. They are extreme optimists in every situation and rarely see or give credence to the hard everyday reality. When you need a boost of positivity, they are like a drink of icy lemonade on a hot Georgia day. You walk away feeling refreshed, encouraged, and ready to tackle the world.

The Advisers are the third category of voices. These people believe in you and want you to succeed. They know you. They understand what makes you tick. They believe you have something significant to contribute to the community. They want you to win because they understand that when you are doing what you ought to be doing, we all benefit. They speak honesty into your life at just the times when you really need it. They will tell you the truth when it hurts because they know it will help. Advisers believe you have purpose in life, and they are working as hard as you are to find your unique role. The Advisers are the voices you need to prioritize.

Have you ever had a person close to you speak words of insight that in retrospect were so obvious, yet you had been blind to them previously? People around me often see more in my life than I can see. Sometimes we are just too close to situations and need others who are just a little removed to see what we don't see. We may have intentionally blinded ourselves, or we may just be unable to see from a particular angle.

If you are the type of person who naturally prefers to make decisions on your own based on intuition, data, lists, or spiritual guidance, you may have some resistance to bringing in Advisers. Maybe you don't like asking for help. Maybe you look around and don't see anyone you trust as much as you trust yourself. Talk with yourself about this. One of the themes that comes up repeatedly in the book of Proverbs is that wise people seek out and listen to counselors, while foolish people don't.

So how do we surround ourselves with people who see the good in us and are willing to contribute to our problem-solving goals?

START WITH THE TABLE

Newlyweds Clay and Maggie set out to build a lifetime of memories together. Believing that the dining room table provides hours of memory-making opportunities, they set out to find the perfect table. Clay searched countless furniture stores and warehouses but always left frustrated. The outrageous cost of the tables they found rarely matched the quality.

Eventually, Clay took matters into his own hands and decided to build Maggie a solid wood table. He researched how to cut, design, and build it, a work of art and love. On the way to building a life, Clay found a way to craft a living. It started as a simple table for his home and turned into a business. Clay's personal passion became his life's work: making tables to make memories.[1] Providing places for families to gather together, stick together, and learn from one another.

Tables are at one level simply places for people to be, but a table is also the place where I have made some of the biggest decisions of my life. At every holiday I sit at tables, sharing a meal with family and playing games late into the evening. I signed the papers to purchase my house at a table. I signed my marriage license at a table. I was sitting at a table when my wife told me she was pregnant. I am currently writing this book at a table. Tables are places of shared stories, friendly advice, and choices confirmed.

Have you ever walked into a conference room with a big table and sat down by yourself for an extended period of time? One of my quirky habits is looking for empty meeting rooms and sitting by myself at conference tables. Next time you see an empty conference room you should try it. Sit at the table and look around at all the different chairs. Some conference rooms have only six chairs, but some are larger and have enough chairs for ten or even twenty people.

Who sits at the conference table of your life? Who do you want at the table with you to make decisions? You have the power to fill the chairs with advocates for you. If you could ask anyone, who would you ask to sit at the table with you? When you are about to make a major decision, who do you want to invite to the table as a special guest? Your life is an open table. Fill it with Advisers.

MAKE THE INVITATION

If you were going to throw a party, but you didn't invite anyone to the table, do you think anyone would show up? No. There wouldn't be anyone at the party to celebrate with you. You will never have people at your table for making choices unless you ask them to sit at your table. There are probably people who you currently know, who play a significant role in your life; and there are people who you don't currently know, but you realize they could contribute a great deal of knowledge toward your future. Who is currently in your community who you need to invite as an adviser for major decisions?

Then, beyond the people you already know well, who can you learn from? These potential advisers may never sit at your table, but they can add value to your future. I always have a list of five to ten people I am trying to connect with and learn from. Some of them I may never meet, as they have a celebrity aspect to their lives and are very difficult to connect with through normal channels or relationships. But surprisingly, through social media many leaders have become very accessible today.

Make a list of ten people you would like to learn from in the coming year. Then think of a strategic way to meet with these people. Have reasons why meeting with them would be beneficial to your future. One great motivational leader did this when he was young. He wrote letters (yes, actual handwritten letters) to leaders and asked them to have lunch with him. He offered them a hundred dollars for the lunch. They nearly always said yes. Sometimes it took a while to get on schedules, but it ultimately happened. Don't expect to get a lunch with a person in a week; it could take months, but just be patient.

I Need Your Advice

As you engage any person to speak into your life, the first phrase you need to learn and include in an invitation to meet with you is, in the words of Dana Lupton, "I need your advice." Dana is the cofounder and executive director of Moving in the Spirit, an empowerment organization that uses dance to teach life principles to urban youth.[2] Dana is a master learner and has built her entire organization on this simple question of creating opportunities for others to speak into her life and work. This positions others as experts and her as the learner. And people love the opportunity to share their wisdom.

When you meet with your advisers, make sure you treat them as if you truly mean you need their advice. Think how frustrated you would be to meet with people, give them advice, and have them combat everything you say with their own perceptions of knowing more. Don't do that. Listen and learn.

Will You Help Me?

Once you get a time to talk with your potential adviser, now you need to be very clear on what you are asking. Always come prepared with some specific questions. I would plan on preparing five to ten questions in advance. A couple of those can be very personal to you here and now. But if you can step back from your current situation and ask a deeper question that gets at broader things that drive decision making, that will be more beneficial to your future. There's a good chance that your adviser may dig down eventually into your specific situation, but start a little broader and glean answers from his or her life experiences before asking questions specifically about your transition or tensions.

Write down what you are learning. Remember, advisers are the experts and you requested the meetings, so treat them as though they are the specialists by listening with attention, turning off your phone, and finishing the meeting early. Treat them with respect and be overly gracious.

What Can I Do for You?

I have had the honor of working with and learning from great visionaries and dreamers. Many of them are great learners and have sat at tables with historic leaders who have changed what life looks like for all of us. Over the years, I have had the opportunity to sit in lunches with these leaders and learn many approaches to connecting with people. One of the greatest things I have learned is a humble way of ending every engagement with another person. Before the meeting is complete, I simply ask, "What can I do for you?"

You will be amazed at how it catches people off guard. Many decision makers are consistently asked for things but rarely asked how the person sitting in front of them could help them. When you ask a question like this, it shifts the conversation from mentorship as a one-way street toward a friendship and colearning conversation. This simple question can turn a meeting from a transaction to a collaborative conversation. Be willing to help others if you are asking for others to help you.

INVITE PEOPLE WHO HAVE WHAT YOU LACK

When I was younger, I played hours of basketball. I am all of five feet six inches tall. In basketball numbers that is short, really short. Some might call it vertically challenged. My best friend growing up was also my height. Though we could play quick, we could never play big. So what did we do? We surrounded ourselves with tall people. Some people call this little-man syndrome; I call it strategic planning.

As teenagers with lots of time on our hands and a love of the game, we would play weekend street basketball tournaments called Gus Macker Basketball. Drawing thousands of people of all ages, we all played to win the official Gus Macker trophy: a basketball-shaped guy with arms and legs and a clever top hat to show he was the king of the court. As I am typing this, I can still hear the song of the tournaments playing in my head. (Luckily I didn't get caught singing that in the locker room.) The tournaments were three-on-three basketball games with each team having one substitute player, so we could all have a break.

To prepare for tournaments, choosing the members of our team was crucial. My friend and I did what any short people would do: we always recruited two big guys to join our team. When I say big, I mean guys who were a minimum of six feet three inches tall. If you can't be tall, recruit tall.

Every tournament, my pastor-turned-coach dad encouraged us to win the sportsmanship award for being respectful of the teams around us and listening to the referee. As the dutiful son that I was, on the first day of the tournament my friend and I would butter up the referee ("Yes, sir!") with the hopes of getting the award before the real competition started on the second day. Once we got that sportsmanship trophy, we were free to talk smack, using the mental game as another tactic to win, because let's face it, we weren't playing to get the sportsmanship trophy—we wanted to win.

Did I mention that we were also very good at talking big even though we were small? I could talk a pretty good game, but my buddy could talk circles around me. Truth be told, our big mouths got us in more fights than I'd like to admit. Most of the time we would find ourselves talking smack while hiding behind our giant friends who could defend us.

The moral of the story: choose the right people to put around you.

INVITE PEOPLE WHO KNOW YOU

We've talked about how to invite people to the table who don't already know you. Now let's consider the people who are close to you.

Some people know us better than others. They stand up with us at our weddings. They show up on the front porch when disaster strikes. They celebrate the victories with us. They know the good in us. They know the bad. And they still want to be our friends. They want us to be successful and will do anything they can to make that happen. We always need these people. The people we drop in to see unannounced, with tears in our eyes, knowing they will sit with us through whatever is happening in that moment. They're not trying to fix us or fix things; they're just present with us in the midst of suffering or celebration.

Who are the three people you would always reach out to in the midst of a major decision? Do they know they matter that much to you? Have you invited them to sit at your table? Write down their names and tell them how much they mean to you. Thank them for being true friends.

Friends are essential, but they're not sufficient. In addition to friends, we also need what I call engaged individuals.

INVITE ENGAGED INDIVIDUALS

Every time I launch a new initiative, I imagine the ideal group of people to be involved in the project. It is usually a combination of my closest friends, the most influential people in the city, and the best-looking, most powerful, and wealthiest individuals in the world. Just a few people with great media and social network followings that could make the idea instantly trend around the world.

I obviously have small expectations. Guess what? That has never happened. The first reality hits when your closest friends are not interested. While you may imagine they would be interested because of their relationship with you, the truth is that they don't always share the same passions. They don't always think your ideas are worth pursuing with their lives. And that's okay. Not every friend will be a business or ministry partner. They can still be friends, and along the way you need friends who are simply friends anyway.

The second thing I have learned time and time again is that the people initially attracted to my new creation are rarely the people expected. In the long run, they are far better, because they actually believe in the idea and they want to contribute, which is better than just believing in me. This is vital to moving forward, because if they want the idea to succeed, they won't just agree with my tactics to keep me happy. The dream should always win over the dreamer. If a dream is only the size of one person, it is not very big at all.

When we started Plywood People, we knew that having a board of directors was essential. So I reached out to some of my closest friends to join me in this new pursuit. I ended up with a group of friends who believed in me, which was a great foundation. The problem was, they weren't everything the organization needed. They supported me, but the organization needed more engaged individuals.

I quickly realized I did not have the right people at the table. All of them were extremely talented, but this wasn't part of their calling. It took three years to transition my board from friends to an actively engaged group. Now the board leads projects, makes connections, thinks objectively about making the organization better, and challenges my ideas to make them the best. They tell me no when they know something else is better for the future of the organization. Changing the people at the table changed the trajectory of our organization.

We need engaged individuals to help us make the best decisions, to lead strategically, to push the organization forward beyond me. People who are invested with time, energy, money, and purpose have the ability to change a question of concern into a pathway of clarity.

INVITE THE POOR TO YOUR TABLE

As I said earlier, one thing about Dr. Martin Luther King Jr. always sticks with me. Every day he was confronted with the most vulnerable people of the city—the poor, hurting, and distressed. He listened to their needs and desires. He had a heart of compassion with the ability to change things. In the same day, he also had the influence to communicate with the most powerful. Whom do you listen to on a daily basis? Do you only listen to the wealthy, or do you have an ear to hear the greatest needs in your community? If your table of voices only has access for the privileged few, your answers will be limited and bend toward positively affecting one community. If you invite the voices of the vulnerable to your table, your opportunity to contribute to changing humanity will be opened to new possibilities.

INVITE THE FUTURE TO YOUR TABLE

It was the biggest conference table I had ever seen. It seated about forty people. It was so big that each seated spot had a microphone sticking up from it so that each person's voice could be amplified to all the other people in the room. It was the conference table for an international network of churches that agree to a series of similar beliefs. I was twenty-two years old at the time, and my boss at the advertising agency I had recently joined had invited me to come along. I wasn't sitting at the table but against the wall in the same room.

The topic of the day was specifically how to engage twentysomethings in the church. On a quick scan of the room, I realized that out of approximately sixty people present I was the only twentysomething. The majority of the room was over the age of fifty. At one point in the discussion, one of the pastors loudly mused, "I wonder what twentysomethings would think about this idea." The entire room turned and looked at me. I was the lone expert. Afterward I laughed about how I was to extrapolate based on the perceptions of everyone aged twenty to thirty around the world.

More important than the question and my answer, though, was my realization that an organization that large had not thought to include any younger generations into their conversation. As they grew older, they had lost perspective on the emerging thought of younger leaders. That experience led me to decide that I would always have interns or young leaders at my table.

It is unfortunately all too common for us to surround ourselves with people who see the world through the same lens we do. This causes us to lose fresh thinking as well as significantly shorten our long-term impact. Innovation often comes from new perspective as well as older wisdom. It's true that young thought will bring naïveté, but that same perspective brings new life. An amazing reciprocation happens when you invite young people to your table. You get the opportunity to pass along advice, and they get the opportunity to introduce you to new thought.

Whom have you invited to the table who brings younger thoughts into your decision making?

LAYERS OF ADVISERS

We need other people to help us make sound decisions. Many choices we have are too difficult to make on our own. As you layer your group of advisers, it will begin to help you make stronger and stronger decisions. Think of it much like the process of making plywood. If you look at the edge of a sheet of plywood, you will notice that it is made of many pieces of wood glued together in a crossing pattern. Its thickness comes from multiple sheets of wood layered together.

Think about all the people at your table who add value to your life. The advisers from different streams of thought will make your choices stronger. They will stand with you in moments of tension and will give you wisdom beyond any you could have imagined. The people you surround yourself with will determine your potential. They will have a direct correlation with the decisions you make in life.

TAKE ACTION

Find an object. Place it on a table. Take away all the chairs from the table. Get a camera. Take photos of that object from every direction possible. Above, below, angles, sides, angles of the object partially in the shot. Adjust the light. Get as artsy as possible. Focus hard to take a hundred different photos of that single object.

Now look through all the different photos. This is what happens when you have people around you who can help you process a major decision. They give you perspective from every imaginable angle. By diversifying the perspective through purposely inviting certain people into your decision-making process, you will find yourself coming to solid and well-informed conclusions.

QUESTIONS FOR GROUPS

1. Who are the people in your life who can be advisers: those who believe in your idea and who will tell you the truth? How receptive are you to inviting their input? Why?

2. Who are five people you would like to learn from in the next year? How easy is it for you to come up with names? How easy is it for you to follow through and ask for their advice? If either of these is hard for you, why do you suppose that's the case?

3. What do you think about inviting the poor to your table? How would that help or not help you in your context? What about inviting the young?

10

SWIMMING TO THE SANDBAR

Name Your Fears

Are you paralyzed with fear? That's a good sign. Fear is good. Like self-doubt, fear is an indicator. Fear tells us what we have to do. Remember one rule of thumb: the more scared we are of a work or calling, the more sure we can be that we have to do it.

Steven Pressfield

On vacation with our best friends on a little island off the gulf coast of Florida, we enjoyed the peaceful location to relax and rejuvenate. The area was most frequently visited by fishermen for seasonal catch. Boats continually came and went while we watched stunning sunsets from our back porch.

One day, my friend Josh and I went for a bike ride and noticed the tide was down in the canal that all the boats used to dock. Boats would come under the bridge and take a strong right turn toward the docks, avoiding a sandbar in the middle. We quickly noticed a handful of people sitting on the sandbar because the tide was so low. The sandbar, with crystal-clear shallow water, looked perfect, and we wanted to join in. They had clearly anchored their boats and swum a short distance. We were on the shore about a hundred yards away. We looked at each other, knowing what we both wanted to do. In a flash, we took off our shoes and shirts, piled them on the beach cruiser bikes we had rented for the week, and raced for the water.

I jumped in first, thinking I could get a jump on Josh. I have known how to swim since I was in second grade, but I have never been a strong swimmer. Josh, on the other hand, is one of those swimmers who looks like he was raised by dolphins. I got out about twenty yards and felt the current pulling me toward the ocean. I quickly realized I was swimming sideways instead of progressing toward the sandbar. I did not see that there was any way I was going to make it, so I turned around and swam back to the shore, fearing being swept out under the bridge and into the ocean.

While I was swimming back, Josh passed me and headed straight toward the sandbar. We both laughed. I caught my breath and walked about fifty yards up the shore to work an angle. By this time, Josh had already arrived on the beach. I jumped in again and made it almost halfway this time when I felt the current pulling me again. Back to the shore I swam. Something about water encompassing my body multiplies my anxiety levels, inhibiting my ability to think, breathe, and move. Fear had set in.

Try again. This time I was visualizing my path to the sand. I knew the trajectory to travel and imagined my arms and legs in a smooth forward motion just like in the videos on YouTube that you can watch for practicing the swim portion of a triathlon. I heard Josh from the sandbar say, "You got this, man! You were so close last time!" Thanks, Josh. If I had grown up with dolphins, I would be on the sand too. I wasn't upset with him, just frustrated with myself.

I jumped in and got ahead of the current. I had never paddled harder in my life than I did in those five minutes. Go. Go. Go. Breathe. Go. Go. Go. Breathe. I'm not going to make it. Keep going. Breathe. I can't breathe. My arms are tired. Keep going. Keep going. Turn around. Fail.

I let fear overtake me again. I went back to the shore. I didn't make it. All in all, I probably swam enough to make it to the sandbar twice but turned around three times in the process. Meanwhile, as Josh was relaxing and finding starfish in the sand, I was sitting on the grass frustrated with my failure. My fear beat out my strength. I had the physical strength to make it across that canal, but I wasn't strong enough mentally.

Fear is my constant companion and my toughest competition. That day in Boca Grande, I let my fear of failure overtake me. I was afraid I wouldn't make it to the sandbar and the current would wash me out to sea. Fear takes many different forms in the process of decision making, and they all result in my not accomplishing the work I was made to complete. Fear brings doubt. Fear leads to quitting. When fear drives my decisions, I usually make the wrong decisions.

When fear succeeds, it shows I don't believe in my personal strengths. I start believing that others would be better at solving the problem. I convince myself that my abilities fall short of others'. Comparison games fill my thinking. These comparisons and mind games don't solve problems; people actually doing the work together and making decisions to push through those barriers do. Decision makers are doers of unthinkable action. They overcome their fears and beat the odds to create progress in a broken world.

Unfortunately, in these moments of doubt, if we let fear win, we retreat from resolution and move in the opposite direction. Just like I did three times in that canal. We turn around and retreat toward the fear, and our only accomplishment is arriving to the safe shoreline to watch the adventure we missed from a distance.

Embarrassment is when your friends witness your greatest fears overtaking you. Yet, if we love our friends, we walk through fears together. In 1 John 4:18, John made this astonishing claim: "Perfect love drives out fear." When we offer unconditional love and stand with our friends, the fear inside each of us is pushed aside. Unfortunately, fear is not going away soon. Because we live in a broken world, fear exists. One day I was reading in Genesis 3 and everything became clear to me. After Adam and Eve had eaten from the tree and God came to find them, they were hiding. God asks Adam why they were hiding and he responds, "I was afraid." It was the first time fear existed and from that time on fear has existed. We all have moments when we are afraid and we will continue to have moments when we are afraid in a broken world. But there is still hope for redeeming and overcoming the things that make us afraid.

As decision makers, we will confront large problems standing between the solution and us. We will want to give up. When I take time to analyze those moments in my past, I realize that more often than not, the barriers were fears within me that I was unwilling to overcome. Josh and I have talked about that day many times since. I've told him how embarrassed I was by the whole situation. He has never made me feel bad about it. We have conspired many times to take a road trip back to that same canal just to swim to the sandbar.

When fears overtake the problems we are called to solve, we miss out on a portion of our unique design. Fears will be prevalent, so we need persistence in beating them. Fears tend to creep in and dominate our potential, but decision makers choose to understand their fears and allow hopeful possibilities to overcome the voice of doubt. I am strong enough to swim across the canal, but my fear was more persistent than my strength. Fear prompted me to quit. Fear removed me from my purpose. We must beat fear with courage even when we don't know where it will take us.

We all doubt that we can become that person who is as unique as we really are. As the *StrengthsFinder* guru Tom Rath stated, "You cannot be anything you want to be—but you can be a lot more of who you already are."[1] Better understanding your giftedness and contribution to the world is hard without overcoming some fears along the way. The alternative is being known by our fears instead of what we courageously pursued. If we don't push through the self-doubt, we will never be known for the problems we are uniquely designed to solve.

Fears hold the most power during decision-making moments. The fears lead to stress, and stress immediately starts attacking the physical body. My fear tenses my shoulders and leaves a permanent set of wrinkles between my eyebrows. Stress raises the blood pressure, deprives us of much-needed sleep, and turns easygoing personalities into anxious overanalyzers. It can keep us from making a decision in any direction, as we choose instead to get lost in the options and the fear of what could happen.

Dr. Ellen Hendriksen, a clinical psychologist at the Stanford School of Medicine, called these moments analysis paralysis. This happens when we overthink a situation to the point of being unable to create movement. We try to get more information to determine the best choice. We research, meet with friends, create lists, procrastinate, check recommendations—anything to put off coming to a conclusion.

Elizabeth Gilbert summed it up clearly: "The problem, simply put, is that we cannot choose everything simultaneously. So we live in danger of becoming paralyzed by indecision, terrified that every choice might be the wrong choice."[2] Never making a choice will result in a life led by fear instead of courage. We are all influenced by fear, but that doesn't mean we must be dominated by fear.

What do you fear? I don't mean fears like the fear of spiders or heights; I mean the fears that keep you from moving toward your purpose. What are the fears you need to overcome? How does a decision maker choose a new path in contrast to that fear? I have experienced and observed seven categories of fears that paralyze us from decisions.

FEAR OF FAILURE

When we are not confident that we will be successful, we don't choose that direction. Erwin McManus believes this fear of failure keeps us from reaching our creative potential. He wrote, "We live in fear of failure, convinced that failure will prove us to be frauds."[3] Potential failure turns big dreamers into non-doers.

My generation was raised on the story of Michael Jordan, one of the greatest basketball players of all time, who failed to make the junior varsity team in high school. He turned failure into a stepping-stone toward his purpose. All of us have the same choice to make. Sadly, we have seen too many images of losing teams and leaders who failed, and we don't want to be the people covering our faces with our suit jackets or jerseys as others watch our humiliation. Fear of failure must be squelched by the possibility of winning. If you make decisions based on a fear of failure, you might as well take yourself out of the game altogether.

Some years ago, I was leading an internal creative team for an event company. I was only twenty-three years old and had been in the position for about four months. We had designed a direct-mail brochure that we were going to send to about 125,000 people. The design was intense with a bunch of information in a small area. The brochure was folded in a unique way to have all the speakers' names on its cover, with more information about them on the inside. The entire printing would cost twenty-five thousand dollars (twenty cents per piece).

I was excited when the brochure returned from the printer and my team and I were checking it out. Every time you get something like that directly from the printer, there is a distinct smell of newness from the ink, and it's easy to dream of the potential of what could happen. One of my teammates blurted out loud, "Does Jim Collins's name have one *l* or two *l*'s?" Two. "Then why is there only one *l* on the cover?"

We had misspelled Jim Collins's name on the cover of the brochure. Jim Collins is one of the best-known business minds in the world. I had to take the brochure to the president of our organization. He looked at it quickly and asked what I thought we should do. Reprint it?

We had to reprint all 125,000 brochures. I'll never forget what he said to me that day: "We all have failures. The difference with people like you and me is that we fail big. Some people spend twenty-five thousand dollars on a master's degree, but you got your degree today. Guess what? You will make a mistake again, you will fail again, but never forget this moment and don't let this failure happen again."

He was gracious when I failed hard and quickly in my new role. A twenty-five-thousand-dollar mistake at the age of twenty-three. He did joke with me as I was leaving his office, reminding me that he could have bought a car for the price of that mistake. It made us both laugh and made me feel worse.

Entrepreneurs are witnessing a positive shift in the discussions about failure. The recent trend is encouraging people to fail as fast as they can. Fail fast—fail often. These people believe the quicker you fail, the more clarity you have for the future. If an idea doesn't work, you know it right away and can move on to a different track.

Without failure we will never understand what we are intended to do or not do. Without failure we will not understand how to make better decisions that line up with our love, story, and dream. Without failure we will never succeed. Failure makes us stronger. Failure is where we learn. Even the wisest of leaders will make wrong choices.

Decision makers fail often and fail fast because we know that even through failures we gain wisdom and get closer to our calling.

FEAR OF THE FUTURE

All of us are risk averse, some more than others. Entrepreneurs tend to be less afraid of risk, but decision-making times heighten our awareness and fear of the uncertainty of the future. A major barrier to making a good decision is focusing too intently on a decision's effect on our future.

We fear losing money and safety because of the security we fictitiously attach to them. We regularly conjure up a false sense of security around where we live, what we drive, where we work, and how much money we have in the bank. The insurance industry is built on our risk-hedging behavior; month after month we pay for life, health, and property insurance. The truth is, regardless of our planning, none of these safety measures can guarantee our future. They are managing the risk of the future, but ultimately we remain uncertain of what will happen tomorrow.

I understand there is a need for insurance and risk management, and I pay for them, but we must honestly examine our fear of tomorrow. There is no certainty in our future. No health insurance can prevent a loved one from getting cancer. Large and small companies shut down suddenly, leaving employees without jobs. One hundred percent security does not exist. We may lose our job, have a tornado hit our house, or tragically lose a close family member at any given time with no explanation. If fear of such events drives how we live, we will allow anxiety to make our choices in order to limit risk, creating fictitious control in life. Charles Lee said, "We can't let insecurity become the justification for not doing something…. The alternative to *not* moving forward is living the life you never wanted."[4]

The fear of an uncertain financial future is a fear that many of us struggle to conquer. I consulted with an event that brought in roughly four million dollars. I could see the organizers needed to make a drastic shift in their approach to stay in front of where culture was heading in their arena, but they chose not to change because of the potential short-term shift in revenue generation. They had built a short-term company perspective dependent on today's four million dollars, and now three years later they are losing money. They let fear drive their decision. The short-term certainty took precedence over long-term purpose.

Decision makers understand that our future is out of our control, and we pursue purpose in spite of the risk.

FEAR OF THE UNKNOWN

No human is good at all things. I'm not sure where the idea of "having it all together" came from, but we have wrongly assumed that it includes knowing everything. The goal is not to have it all together or know it all; the goal is to know where we are going and to have the confidence to move toward that end. Problem solvers will continually run into things they don't understand, areas outside their expertise. This is an opportunity to admit ignorance or weakness and look to others for assistance.

We need others to help us make our dreams happen. Admitting this is terrifying to many. It is also one of the dividing lines between those who succeed and those who fail. Most of our greatest limitations are within us, so the quicker we realize that we don't know everything, the quicker we can rely on others' giftedness. Let me tell you about a friend who succeeded only because she allowed others to help her.

Have you ever eaten a macaron? I had never tasted one until I met Xanna, who was only nineteen years old at the time. Macarons are two delicate cookies with cream in the middle. I think of them as a cross between an Oreo and a cupcake, surpassing both in flavor and texture. Xanna loved macarons and was always on the lookout for them throughout the Atlanta area.

When she finally found the perfect one, it cost $3.50—for one! That's a lot of money for a two-inch-diameter cookie, so she decided to learn to make them herself and share them with friends. They were so delicious, her friends began asking if they could pay her to make more. Before she knew it, she was in the bakery business, selling macarons. Two months later she was getting close to fifty dozen orders per week. She started with a love and the love spread.

As it took more of her time and energy, she realized that she was creating a business. She had instinctively started a business without knowing anything about running one. She had just one problem: she was not making money. As her love met with success, she saw the potential. Seeing the opportunity to continue doing what she loved as her job, she realized she was going to have to make some money.

I connected Xanna to an accountant named Chet. Chet sat with her for two hours and helped her realize the true cost of her product and what she needed to charge to start making money. Because she had asked for help, Xanna, Chet, and I joyfully celebrated a new bakery venture called XK Macarons.[5] If she had been driven by fear of what she didn't know, hiding in that fear rather than seeking out the counsel she needed, I would not be enjoying those sweets today and she would not be doing this job that she loves.

Xanna, like many experts in their chosen fields, didn't know how to do accounting; she only knew how to make macarons. She just needed to know Chet, the accountant. For everything we don't know, there is someone else whose strength is exactly what we don't know. The key is to find those people and integrate them into our decisions.

Decision makers choose to focus on what we do know and find others to fill the unknown spaces in order to keep moving forward.

FEAR OF CHANGE

We want change, but we don't want to change. This is why every gym is full of people the first week of January and the regulars breathe a sigh of relief by mid-February. We all know we need to change, but we don't want to do the hard work that change requires. Change happens when people choose a different way. We want to lose weight but don't want to change our diet. We want clean clothes but don't want to do the laundry. We want a partner in life but don't want to change our individual habits. We are scared of what change means for us.

Change is always attractive if it benefits us while guaranteeing us not to suffer. This fear of the suffering in the midst of change causes many people to retreat from the decision. But change brings new hope and life to broken situations. Father Gregory Boyle, the Jesuit priest who works with gang members in Los Angeles, developed a mature understanding of the nature of change: "There is nothing 'once and for all' in any decision to change. Each day brings a new embarking. It's always a recalibration and a reassessing of attitude and the old, tired ways of proceeding, which are hard to shake for any of us."[6] Problem solvers require change to solve problems. We choose to tackle the fear of change, starting with changing ourselves not just once but day after day.

Decision makers believe that if change is going to happen, it starts with us choosing a new way one day and continuing to choose it day after day.

FEAR OF CRITIQUE

Every moment of tension we meet with a decision will be followed by a critique. Critique can take the form of personal regret, dissatisfied customers or coworkers, or a random blog comment from a person we have never even met. Usually I am my own worst critic. In hindsight, I second-guess my own choices all the time.

You may think of decisions you have made in the past, both personally and professionally, and ask yourself, "What was I thinking?" Or you may remember choices you made that others criticized, asking, "What were you doing?" You may regret a choice you made to marry the person you did or to cheat on your spouse. You may regret making the move across the country away from your family or signing the thirty-year mortgage on your house. You may regret choosing to stay in the profession you are currently in or not choosing to stay with the job you liked much more than your current one.

All these regrets are married with criticism in your head that send you the message that you are not good enough. You may be fearful that someone is going to call you out on all those things, pointing out your failures and sticking them in your face. You may fear that you have not lived up to someone else's expectations for your life. It may be someone you love, your parents, mentors, or close friends you feel you have disappointed.

Tom Paterson is a life coach and leading thinker in creating life plans. He said, "Anytime someone lives primarily to fulfill expectations of another person—rather than to fulfill the precise and unique purpose of God—that person is going to be miserable, unfulfilled and less than whole. Anger, resentment, bitterness, and hate are very likely to manifest themselves—some of which may be expressed outwardly, but all of which will burrow deep within and destroy the person from the inside out."[7] We can't meet expectations at all times, and if we choose to apply expectations to our lives, we won't be fulfilled. If we choose to believe that we have failed to fulfill the expectations of others, then we ultimately believe we are not enough.

I can have a hundred great reviews and one negative critique, and the only voice I hear is the critique. We want to be loved and accepted by others, and critics push against that feeling. Critiques hang in the back of my mind nearly all the time, and for good reason. Critics will always be present. Every person doing something significant will be confronted with opposing opinions. Though we know the haters will hate, somehow knowing that truth does not make it easier when the haters hate me.

My wife and I spoke at a college a year ago for a total of six times over the course of seven hours in one day, and we loved it. Interacting with students is always a joy because we try to share things we have learned on our life journey with the hope that our stories will encourage and guide their journey. The next day I received a call from one of the leaders. He gave me a very disappointing critique. He told me I was selfish and he was unimpressed with how I presented myself to the students. I have known this man for many years and I was devastated. Was I selfish? Were my motives wrong? Did I not live up to his expectations? I will never forget that phone call, and now when I speak, there is a nagging fear within me that I won't live up to the expectations of others.

In every crowd there will be a critic. In every community there will be a doubter. I have come to realize that most people who try to bring others down have been held back personally because of fear within their souls that they could not break through; so now they try to bring others down also.

Decision makers will not be held back by the potential criticism of others. We fight through criticism to create something in this world.

FEAR OF REJECTION

We don't want others to say no to us. The sooner we realize that behind every yes are always several nos, the sooner we can walk past a no to get to the yes. All of us will hear the word *no* at some point in our journey, and that's not a reason to be held back with fear.

Jia Jiang decided to do a social experiment called one hundred days of rejection therapy.[8] His aim was to make one hundred crazy requests, fully expecting to hear the word *no*. His goal was to desensitize himself to the pain of rejection and overcome his fear in the process. He had three criteria for his experiment: (1) ethical (no lying or marriage undermining); (2) legal (the request had to obey the laws of the land); and (3) doesn't defy the laws of physics.

Some of his requests were pretty extreme. He asked for a burger refill at a restaurant. He requested to give the weather forecast on live TV. Instead of checking out a mattress for five minutes at a Mattress Firm, he asked to stay all night. He even had the guts to request an interview with President Obama. What was unexpected, though, was how many people said yes! They answered yes to his crazy requests: a policeman let him drive his car; he got custom Krispy Kreme doughnuts in the shape of the Olympic rings.[9]

If we are driven by the fear of rejection, we are letting negative potential overtake the possibility of our future.

Decision makers don't fear rejection; we look past the no in search of the yes.

FEAR OF BEING KNOWN

What happens if everything works out? Then people might really know me, and I don't want them to know everything about me.

Inevitably, successful people go through a period when the worst things about them are revealed. It's the classic VH1 story of the famous person revealing his or her dark side. If people really knew everything about you, would they still like you? Will your darkness negate all the good you are trying to accomplish? This fear permeates all of us.

It's one reason why it's so difficult to become the president of the United States. Political parties have resorted to looking for younger leaders to nominate, hoping they have less dirty laundry than those who have lived longer. Success brings spotlights, and many people are fearful of what that would do to them, their families, and other relationships.

Decision makers know there are no perfect people and choose to focus on our giftedness rather than bringing others down. We champion and support others, knowing each of us needs grace in one area or another.

ENGLISH AVENUE

Every year, Plywood People holds an innovation idea competition, asking for submissions of problem-solving ideas to compete for twenty-five thousand dollars in funding and services. Our board of directors reads through all the submissions and narrows them down to the top five ideas. The finalists then share at our annual event for social innovators called Plywood Presents. Each presenter gets five slides and five minutes to share his or her big idea. It's a platform of over six hundred people and an opportunity to present the idea to a wider audience.

Laura Pritchard-Compton was selected as one of the final five for her project called Urban Perform. Before her presentation I invited her to our office so I could listen to her big idea in person. I sat down at my desk and asked her to present in front of me. Sometimes presenting in front of one person is more difficult than sharing in front of six hundred. Her face reddened. "You want me to do it right now in front of you?" Yes. I started my phone's stopwatch. Go.

Urban Perform began with Laura's English Avenue neighbors wanting a safe place for exercise. This community is a developing area on the west side of Atlanta, impacted strongly by poverty and its accompanying social issues. Physical health is a primary community concern. Laura has a background in health training and loves physical fitness. Her experience and passion matched her community's need, and she started offering basic fitness classes to students through an after-school program. She quickly expanded to Zumba and nutrition classes, even boot camps. In the fall of 2012, indoor cycling (spin) classes began multiple days a week. And in September of 2013, six students completed their very first triathlon.[10]

She shared her story with me that day and then again a few weeks later, in front of our community, and received an overwhelming response of support. Not surprisingly, Urban Perform was chosen as one of our winners. Beyond our financial support, Laura also has relationships with professional athletes who have contributed to the idea with money and expensive equipment for the gym. Every indicator pointed to Laura's unique gifting for this work.

Laura and I continued to talk about how to move forward. Up to this point, she had been doing all of this as a volunteer. She was coming to me to discuss how to find someone to hire to lead the organization. I was stunned. I point-blank asked her why she wanted someone else to lead instead of her. She didn't know how to respond.

I arranged a dinner for her to meet two friends of mine, Rick and Lynn. Rick and Lynn love to support young entrepreneurial minds and have a gift of helping people see how they can live out their dreams in sustainable ways. Every time I set up a meeting like this for Rick, I make sure the table is covered with paper. As Rick thinks, he writes ideas, bullet points, and action plans until over the course of two hours he basically has a business plan with multiple options covering an entire table. Time and time again, I have watched him clear the table at the end of a meal, fold up the piece of paper, and give it as homework to the dreamer. He is the type of mentor who listens, challenges, and gives action steps. This dinner was no different.

Through the conversation, Rick and Lynn pinpointed the problem: fear. Laura was fearful of the next step, trying every way possible to shrink from the responsibility of being the person she was made to be. Her decisions were driven by two fears: fear of the future and fear of the unknown. First, we hadn't known this before, but Laura had learned that she and her husband were expecting a baby. This news brought a series of new tensions. Second, she didn't want to ask for help. She didn't feel comfortable asking for money from others to support her. She had no trouble asking supporters to donate to the project, but not to her livelihood. Admitting *she* needed others' help felt like an entirely different thing. Her fears were determining her future.

Laura walked away from the dinner with a tabletop full of decisions. She had to choose to overcome her fears in order to do what she was made to do. One year later, she has birthed her baby and has been given a building for the gym and personal financial support to make Urban Perform her job. Laura is doing what she ought to be doing. She is a decision maker who chose not to be held back by her fears. She jumped in and took a swim to the other side of the canal.

Fears will always be present; they surround us, push us, tug at us, and try in every way possible to bring us down, but they will not beat us. When you stand up when fear fights to take you down, when you walk through the fear with others, when you choose your purpose over fear, it makes you stronger.

Decision makers fail often and fail fast because we know that even through failures we gain wisdom and get closer to our calling. Decision makers understand that our future is out of our control, and we pursue purpose in spite of the risk. Decision makers choose to focus on what we do know and find others to fill the unknown spaces in order to keep moving forward. Decision makers believe that if change is going to happen, it starts with us choosing a new way one day and continuing to choose it day after day. Decision makers will not be held back by the potential critiques of others. We fight through criticism to create something in this world. Decision makers do not fear rejection; we look past the no in search of the yes. Decision makers know there are no perfect people and choose to focus on our giftedness rather than bringing others down. We champion and support others, knowing each of us needs grace in one area or another.

TAKE ACTION

As I write this, I have had multiple conversations with Josh about that canal. My hope is that by the time this book is published I will have swum across the current and stood on the sandbar with Josh. My challenge to you is to think about what fears you most identify with. Think about a scenario where that fear overtook your decisions. Share that story with one other person you trust so he or she can help you move through that fear the next time it holds you back.

QUESTIONS FOR GROUPS

1. Which fear discussed in this chapter is the most powerful for you? How has it held you back?

2. What did you read in this chapter that helped you overcome a fear?

3. What is one step you could take to confront or act in spite of a fear? What help will you need?

11

THE QUIET IN
THE STORM

Make Time for Solitude

Only by being detached from created things can
we make good choices about them, so that we can
achieve the end for which we are created.

Jim Manney

Our family was in Pittsburgh, Pennsylvania, for an event with a few thousand college students. One of the clearest memories I have from our hotel on that trip is the challenge of getting an elevator, because we were on the twenty-first floor and there were countless students fighting for access to the lobby. Our daughter was taking her afternoon nap, and my wife wanted to go for a run. (She was training for her first marathon.) I decided to stay in our hotel room during nap time and get some work done in a dark room with the soothing ambiance of a sound machine.

It's very common for Andre to map her run before running in a new place, to be sure she gets the distance she needs. To southerners, Pittsburgh in February is remarkably cold. Snow covered the ground, and the air was cold enough to create a spurt of steam with every breath. About twenty minutes into Andre's ten-mile run, I received a call. The track she had mapped for her run had a major change; one of the roads dead-ended where a bridge was out. She had tried changing direction, only to be blocked by further city construction. Every place she turned, she met with a dead end. She was lost and had run out of options for where to go next.

Navigation innovators have provided increasingly useful and detailed tools so that we always know where we are in relation to the rest of the world. It started with a compass, moved to maps, then radically transformed with the advances of technology. Modern GPS tools tell us where we are, allow us to choose where we want to be, and give us remarkably detailed instructions for every step in between. We can even follow an electronic voice that warns us when a turn is coming and modifies the path when we take a wrong turn.

If we lose a technology device, we can find it on a different digital mapping device and track where it lands. We can control our heating and cooling system from our phone or even watch a webcam to monitor the security of our home. Technology tools tell us which friends are near and what hotels, restaurants, and stores are giving the best deals. Finding what to do next, seeing what is around us, and getting directions have never been easier. The downside is that we have lost the art of making decisions on our own and listening for direction from something greater than technology.

Andre was still running (with no clear direction, as her technology had failed her during this crisis) and talking to me through her headphones. An application on her phone gave me the ability to track her exact location on my computer with a little blinking dot on a map. She still needed to run an additional seven miles and get back to the hotel room. For the next hour, I talked her through the entire run. She was my eyes on the road, and I was tracking her progress through the app. We were a great high-tech team, using the resources at hand to conquer each challenge as it arose. It felt like we were in a movie and I was directing a high-speed chase. (Of course, the "high speed" was a ten-minute-mile pace.)

This experience was bringing Andre and me together in such a unique way. She needed me for high-level direction and major turns; I needed her to let me know what challenge was coming ahead. Toward the end of the journey, I told her confidently to turn left on the next street, as it was the only way back to the hotel. Exhausted, she turned left and stopped in her tracks, yelling into her device, *"Are you kidding me? That's the steepest hill I have ever seen in my life!"* As she trudged up the hill, I recited all the most profound motivational quotes I could remember from my childhood basketball coaches. She ran up that hill and ultimately made it back to the hotel. Cue victorious movie soundtrack.

She was lost and needed some guidance. She didn't know what to do; she was seeking a voice with a perspective different from hers for guidance on where to go next. What do you do when you don't know what to do?

GETTING LOST

In moments of choice, it's important to separate yourself from the situation. Solitude offers you the space to clarify your thoughts and seek guidance from a perspective greater than human wisdom. While I don't even come close to being that voice, Andre's running adventure that day provided me with a real-life experience of what happens when we need God. When we are lost, we need to be found, and there is only one voice that can both comfort and direct.

When was the last time you were lost? It seems rare that we get lost anymore. With GPS services we have created a way to always be in control of our directions. Technology has caused us to lose our reliance on God. We have replaced God's divine presence with the devices in our hands. In the original Garden of Eden, man and woman were naked until they fell. Now I feel naked if I don't have car and house keys in my front pocket, my wallet in my back pocket, and my phone in hand. In theory and practice, with those three things I can buy anything, get anywhere, and find answers to life's most difficult questions.

We create lives that separate us from our need for God. Yet we need a higher perspective more than our habits allow. We need moments of solitude to reframe our thinking. By taking those moments consistently, we need to integrate our reliance on God into our ongoing lives.

Pastor Dave Gibbons leads communities all over the world and is a spiritual mentor for hundreds of leaders. I had the opportunity to interview him and another pastor he mentors from Chicago. Dave had recently taken him to Thailand for a spiritual time away from his team. We tend to equate these retreat times with the spiritual practices of prayer, fasting, and study, but Pastor Dave had another spiritual practice in mind. Get lost. Get lost? Yes. No map; no guide. In an unfamiliar country with a foreign language, get lost. He was to walk the streets for hours with the purpose of exploring and relying only on God, not technology, for direction, entertainment, and communication.

Dave has realized something that we instinctively know but don't want to tackle. We daily rely on the voices of others to guide our next step, but we have lost our ability to trust in God. He challenges people to regain a reliance on God for next steps. He forces people to think about what they want to do and what God wants them to do. They don't choose a restaurant based on others' recommendations; they find something that looks good. They relight the spark of curiosity, learning to explore firsthand the good, true, and beautiful.

TEACHING OURSELVES TO STOP

The practice of stopping has been lost to the efficiency of modern life. We don't have time to stop. We don't have time to pray. At one time my normal workday included a lunch break; now I always work through lunch. I used to stop and give thanks for the food I was about to eat, but I've lost that act of thankfulness due to drive-throughs and eating while doing. Break time gets filled with Internet searching or documentation of my life on social media to share with others.

I believe in order to think holistically we must reteach ourselves to stop. We must detach from connectivity and proactively choose a moment to slow progress and think about what we ought to do instead of what we can do. In times of tension and transition, we need to find still moments.

To experience a still moment, we often need to leave the modern world and enter the created world. We need to feel the wind blow through our hair on a mountaintop, walk in the grass with no shoes on, and drink from a natural spring-fed lake. If you live in a city, when was the last time you saw the stars in the sky? A still moment separates us from reason, fear, and time, while connecting us to the Creator.

I have even found great stillness while taking a shower. There is something about the uninterrupted movement of water that spawns clarity. In the stillness is where we gain direction from God. This is when we give ourselves an opportunity to open our decisions to God.

We have the modern convenience of gaining all the research possible at a moment's notice, but that information rarely answers our deepest questions and concerns. To get guidance from God, we have to begin to engage God again as a spiritual practice.

JESUS'S MODEL

In Mark 1:35, we learn about Jesus's practice of solitude as an important spiritual exercise: "Very early in the morning, while it was still dark, Jesus got up, left the house and went off to a solitary place, where he prayed." Where is your solitary place? Sometimes we need to create a place to be alone to rely on something larger for our reason for being.

A litmus test to know if we need some alone time is when we are surrounded with people and yet feel lonely. This is when we need to actively select solitude to be reminded of a greater Love.[1]

The practice of going to a solitary place, as Jesus exemplified time and time again, is a lost discipline in a culture created to increase efficiency and action. If we pursue action apart from solitude, our decisions will be hurried and lack patience. When the outside demands increase, and more and more people are requesting my presence or my advice, I sometimes reason that I don't have time for this solitary period. Yet when Jesus was in the throes of His brief three years of active ministry, crowds following His every move, people lining up to be healed, the Scriptures share that Jesus was committed to frequent moments of stillness and prayer.

After healing many diseases in people, Jesus sneaked away (Luke 4:42). After He healed a man of leprosy, "Jesus often withdrew to lonely places and prayed" (Luke 5:16). Later, "Jesus went out to a mountainside to pray, and spent the night praying to God" (Luke 6:12). Following that time of prayer, He chose the twelve disciples. I believe that moment of solitude was to gain clarity of choice, to choose His inner circle well.

In Luke 9:18, "Jesus was praying in private." In Luke 21–22, Jesus repeatedly left the crowds to pray and sleep on the Mount of Olives. Jesus showed us the importance of solitude at our times of heightened work pace and decision making. It's true that we aren't trying to feed five thousand or heal the sick every day, but we are trying to make what is broken on earth restored, which is our personal contribution to a much larger story. We need to take note of the spiritual practice Jesus showed us throughout His work, to consistently separate from the crowds and stress of decisions to center our minds and hearts on what we are called to do and who we are called to be.

We often have knowledge that moves us toward choice, but in a society filled with information, decisions without spiritual clarification through solitude frequently lead to misguided actions and unfulfilled expectations. We must retreat to understand true north in a culture moving toward synchronization of choice, a synchronization where all choices are quantified, tracked, and categorized. Without input from God, we are all searching for answers in the same places, getting the same answers, losing our individuality. It's a new form of injustice, the injustice of calling, where we are told through mass media, organizations, and education what we ought to be, instead of hearing God lead us to our true self.

Our true self is always greater than what we are expected to be; it transcends our past mistakes and unfortunate choices. Putting people in boxes based on societal norms and standardized testing can result in a large percentage of people not following their true callings. We must continue to seek God through the process or we may get swept along in the current of life.

THINK TIME

Bill Gates practiced a similar concept of "think time."[2] When he led Microsoft, twice per year he would separate himself from family, friends, and employees for a week to ponder the future direction of the company. Beforehand, he would ask employees for ideas of where this technology company could go in the future and to submit white papers documenting their ideas. He would then review over a hundred concepts every "think week" and consider new directions for the company. He would also respond in that time to each of the ideas. He learned the art of separating himself from the crowd to gain clarity in how to move forward.

We need to schedule times to think. We may not all have the luxury of taking two weeks off annually just to ponder the future, but we can take an hour or two consistently even on a workday to gain clarity as a decision maker. Step away from the situation and gain a broader perspective on the problem.

Making big decisions with clarity in solitude will not just happen. You have to practice working through the small decisions in those quiet moments first. No matter the size of your choice, the practice of submission to God creates a path toward good choices. It reminds us of our place on earth. It creates humility of spirit and helps us realize just how little we know and how much we need Him.

When I separate myself to think about choices at hand, I try to process problems through a series of questions to lead toward resolution.

1. Where Am I?

Once I get alone and have time to think, two things consistently happen to me. Stillness equally generates exhaustion and creation. First, I quickly realize how tired my mind and body are. Don't be surprised if you fall asleep. Sometimes the greatest decisions happen only after resting your body, so if this is what you need, by all means sleep. Second, my imaginative mind takes over. Ideas start bouncing around my head like vending machine bouncy balls. Often these thoughts have no connection with the problem directly in front of me.

Here is the moment when I ask myself a simple question: Where am I? I begin to talk to myself about all the places my mind is zipping off to and draw those thoughts back to the humble place of seeking direction. It's okay for our minds to wander for a moment, but bring focus and direction back to your time of solitude. It can be helpful to have a short phrase or physical motion to stop this distraction. As a random thought or worry arises, simply say, "And this I give to You, Jesus." As you do, you can use your hands to physically hand it over.

To continue to open my heart and mind to God's guidance, this prayer from the Book of Common Prayer has been helpful for me:

> O God, by whom the meek are guided in judgment, and light riseth up in darkness for the godly: Grant us, in all our doubts and uncertainties, the grace to ask what thou wouldst have us to do, that the Spirit of wisdom may save us from all false choices, and that in thy light we may see light, and in thy straight path may not stumble; through Jesus Christ our Lord. Amen.

2. How Ought It to Be?[3]

Perhaps the most difficult piece of being a problem solver is that authentic problem solvers live in the middle of the problem. While surrounded with the pressures and tensions of the problem, we can lose sight of how it is supposed to be. Leaving the daily tension to find a place of rest offers us the chance to once again remember the goal. What are we working toward? How is it supposed to be? Leaving behind the intricacies of daily living frees our imaginations and our souls to once again envision the beauty of what could be.

Sometimes that starts with envisioning who we can be. We may have lost a piece of ourselves in the midst of the turbulence. We can start by asking God, "What ought to be in me?" Take the time to let Him restore peace, or creativity, or passion once again. Then we can move more wholly toward how it ought to be in our unique problem-solving situation. We can consider questions like: If the problem did not exist, what would things look like? If we work toward the solution, what will our community look like?

This is a great time to use paper and pen to keep you focused and dream with clarity. I always bring a journal on these times of solitude. Leave behind the technology and remember what it feels like to hold a pen again. Sketch a picture or write the words of the ideal once again. Let the ideal rebuild what gets stripped away in the day-to-day work of problem solving.

3. What Would You Have Me Do?

Once you have restored the wonder of the greater task you are trying to accomplish, you can ask God to give you more specific direction. I want to be able to tell you that the minute you pray and seek divine intervention there will be an amazing, lightning-bolt experience that will give you direction, but chances are that won't happen. You may or may not hear a voice or see a light, but many, many people throughout time have attested to having their thoughts guided by God when they take time to seek Him.

Limit your expectations, but give yourself time to dwell in the moment. You may sit for ten minutes or ten hours before clarity for your next steps comes to you. There is no formula for answers in these most difficult moments, but by going through all the elements of becoming a decision maker, you will make a more informed decision.

All the questions you have thought through are a means for answers, but the questions don't always give the answers. My sister often speaks of God giving her directions that have more to do with how to do something than what exactly to do. As she prays, she hears that she is to choose joy or give kindness. These instructions remind us that it is not always what we do but how we do it that will influence others in powerful ways.

In Proverbs 3:5–6, Solomon instructs us to "trust in the LORD with all your heart and lean not on your own understanding; in all your ways submit to him, and he will make your paths straight." To walk along a path, we must take a series of hundreds of steps. We must have belief that God has control of the long journey and will continue to guide us in the right direction. That doesn't mean that He will intervene in each unique choice; rather, I think it means that He will keep us headed in the direction toward the right end.

Sometimes we are choosing between two great options. I think in those moments there is no wrong choice. We choose one and move forward confidently. Seek God in these moments of stillness and trust there is a larger story unfolding that we will see someday. Louie Giglio said it this way: "God is using your present circumstances to make you more useful for later roles in His unfolding story." Take time to trust that God has a glimpse of the entire path and the decisions you are making today will help play an even more significant role in the future.

4. What Am I Going to Do?

You know what your decision-making style is. You have thought through all the possible options. You have asked for guidance from trusted advisers. You have taken the time to seek God. Now it is time to make a choice. Andy Stanley posed a remarkable question in his book *The Best Question Ever;* "In light of your past experience, current circumstances, and future hopes and dreams, what is the wise thing for you to do?"[4]

This is the point where you need to decide. This is where that journal and pen once again become important. Maybe you write one word that brings clarity on how to move forward. Maybe you write out every thought on paper, feeling again what it is like to have aching fingers, but working your thoughts through to a decision. This is the time to decide what you think is the best choice given all the information you have been given. Make a decision and write it down. Remember, we can never be sure of what is going to happen in the future; so given all the information you have received, what will you do?

In chapter 3, I talked about Plywood Retreats, when about fifteen people come together with problems to solve. As I said, on day two of the three-day retreat we collect each person's technology devices and force them to retreat for a two-hour time of solitude. They leave feeling stressed about all they have learned and uncertain of how they should move forward. They return not with all the answers, but with a sense of peace and openness in their minds to the possibilities that lie ahead.

One of the spaces we encourage our social innovators to experience during their time of solitude is the labyrinth, located deep in the woods. As you walk the faint path to reach it, you find yourself feeling like you are wandering into a magical far-off land. If you have never experienced a labyrinth, it is simply a man-made spiral-patterned maze. This labyrinth begins outside the circle and slowly draws you to the center of the spiral maze. As you walk the labyrinth, you move sometimes closer and sometimes farther from the center of the design.

The labyrinth is intended to be a prayer journey that calms your mind and causes you to focus on God. The labyrinth we use is constructed with fairly large rocks. The entire space is easily seventy feet in diameter and can take as fast as ten minutes or longer than two hours to walk through, depending on your pace and the feelings you are working through. The labyrinth is a sacred space in which to be quiet and ponder, to listen to God and slow down your decision making. Sometimes when you walk into the design, you just want to hop over the rocks and find the shortcut to the center because it's difficult to slow yourself down and enjoy the process. However, that's the point. Slow down. Put one foot in front of the other. Walk slowly. Breathe deeply. Meditate on your journey. Take the time you need to focus and listen to God's leading.

When people experience this time of quiet, we can physically see the stress of their decisions melt away. Everyone finds peace in quieting their mouths and seeking guidance from God. At the end of the two hours, we rejoin and sit in a circle. I rarely need to say a thing because people are excited to share their moments of clarity. When we proactively choose to experience stillness, clarity comes.

TAKE ACTION

This week, get lost at work. Open up your calendar and plan a two-hour block of time to get lost. Schedule it. Leave your phone on your desk. Walk out the front door and go for a walk by yourself, letting your mind wander for a bit. If your work does not allow for this type of creative thinking and downtime, plan on it over the weekend. See things you haven't seen before. Look for the good, true, and beautiful in your environment.

Remember, you don't need to share it through social media. Just admire it and be reminded of the Creator. Go through the process above to seek God's direction in your life. There may be a big decision you need to make or a relationship that needs to be addressed. Just get lost for a couple of hours and see what happens. See how it transforms the rest of your day. Take a journal and write down what you ought to do next in life.

QUESTIONS FOR GROUPS

1. What role does solitude have in your life? What motivates you to make time for solitude? What gets in the way? What could help you address those obstacles?
2. How does technology affect your reliance on God? How does busyness affect it?
3. Do you think you need to rely on God more? Why or why not? How do you respond to the idea of asking God what you should do—not just once in a while, but on a regular basis?

12

A RUN ON THE BELTLINE

Step Forward

We should live and labor in our time that what came to us
as seed may go to the next generation as blossom, and that
which came to us as blossom may go to them as fruit.
Henry Ward Beecher

Life is a collection of every choice we make woven together in a timeline and documented through our memory and the memories of others. Every time we say yes or no to something, it takes us in a direction toward some things and away from others. We choose what we will be for and what we will be against. Though today's decision may feel like one of the most difficult we have ever processed, it is taking us further down a path, preparing us for tomorrow's decision, which will probably be even more difficult.

While some decisions are easier than others and some dreams are larger than others, I believe each decision we face makes up who we are. Our story, our love, and our dreams combine to create each person to be a unique decision maker. Decision makers choose to love others, share their story with others, and solve problems every day that contribute to making things better for others. Decision makers are composed of the thousands of choices they make every day, propelling them forward in a positive motion, creating momentum for others to join.

Decision makers don't happen in a day; they happen every day. Every day we become better at making decisions, and every day we have the opportunity to gain wisdom in the journey. Decisions don't happen in a moment; they happen continuously. Decisions won't go away.

As we build our portfolio, we gain opportunities to make even more important decisions and even advise others. The start of this exciting journey is to make the next decision. When we have a sense of where we are going, the best way to get there is to take the next step.

THE GUY BEHIND THE BELTLINE

When I think about the long-term nature of a vision marked by the painstaking work of day-by-day decisions, I always think of the BeltLine in Atlanta. My family and I regularly enjoy the beginning phases of the BeltLine, biking or walking the path and soaking in the sun and beauty at a connected neighborhood park, but this is only the tip of the iceberg in terms of the many benefits planned for this huge undertaking. Once it is completed, the BeltLine will encircle the city of Atlanta in a twenty-two-mile loop of rail and transportation connecting forty-five urban neighborhoods and encompassing green space, housing, and art. Here is the vision: "The beauty of the Atlanta BeltLine is that … it is a living, breathing part of our community; not simply a means of getting somewhere, but a destination unto itself. It offers a chance for Atlanta to redefine what it is to be a neighbor, to be a community, to be a region, and to share all that it has to offer."[1]

After reading about the man behind the vision, I decided it was time to meet Ryan Gravel. I wanted to hear firsthand the steps that led to his decision to pursue such an outrageous project. We met early in the morning in the basement café of a restaurant in a neighborhood called Inman Park. He was riding his bike to work and agreed to let me buy him a cup of coffee. He began by sharing his great fascination with railroads and the role trains have played in the constructed design of cities. In the late 1990s, while he was a college kid at Georgia Tech hoping to become an urban planner, he started exploring the west side of the city, an industrial community with many rail lines. A historic map revealed a railroad line that created a circle inside the city. He researched further and found a twenty-two-mile loop of train track, overgrown and essentially hidden. The BeltLine rail line was not usable anymore, but he wondered what could be done with these twenty-two miles of contiguous space.

He traveled for a year abroad in Paris and lived near an old abandoned rail line. It was under reconstruction during the time he lived there into the Viaduc des Arts, and when he returned one year later, he found a community transformed. The Viaduc is now a major center for the arts and crafts, with fifty craft workers exercising their talents in a variety of professions linked to fashion and decoration. If you visit, you'll find lighting manufacturers, furniture restorers, shopkeepers selling old frames and prints, and fashion, jewelry, and accessory designers.[2] The old railroad was transformed into a garden called the Promenade Plantee, which became the inspiration for the High Line in New York City, and it ultimately inspired Ryan to envision what could happen with the BeltLine.

He started to concept the possibilities of what this old railroad could become for Atlanta: "It was interesting to dream about occupying a space that didn't currently exist to the public." This idea became his thesis completed in 1999. He never intended for the thesis to happen in real life—he just wanted to finish school—but the idea always nagged at the corners of his mind.

Ryan had many late evening discussions with friends about the idea, but he never believed it would really come to fruition. Two years later, he was working on an architecture project that was adjacent to the BeltLine property, and it caused him to rethink what could be. He was designing the development and pondering if part of the design should open up to the BeltLine property. He had deeper conversations with two friends. "If they had not encouraged and driven the next steps, it would have never happened; there was no way." They not only pushed it; they did it.

Ryan's friend Sara decided that they should write letters to everyone important in the city who could potentially push the BeltLine project forward in some capacity. The letter-writing party began. She believed it was worth asking. The answer would either be yes or no. The worst-case scenario was no. The best-case scenario was the BeltLine coming to life.

They received mostly defeating letters and a lot of nos. But one person said yes: Cathy Woolard, chair of the transportation committee for city council. She thought if this idea had the potential to help with Atlanta traffic, it was worth a conversation.

For two and a half years, Ryan and Cathy and others gave speech after speech to any community in Atlanta that would listen. Using a projection slideshow during their presentations, they literally clicked through all the pictures of the possibilities and plans for the BeltLine. Throughout this pursuit, Ryan was not paid for three years; he simply loved having conversations about green space, transportation, commerce, and unifying communities. He asked, "How do we construct and build in this world, while being a person living in it?" His love mixed with his story, and a dream drove his decision to keep moving forward, to keep taking the next step.

The turning point came one evening while he was standing outside prepping for a speech. He overheard two women say two words: "our BeltLine." They used that phrase multiple times as they chatted. Suddenly he truly believed that the BeltLine was going to happen. He knew it deep in his soul. That moment made every previous grueling choice worth the work. It wasn't going to be the original dream he had conceptualized—the change has come through an expansion of the vision beyond anything they could have imagined in the beginning and it is better than the first idea. It was more significant because "they wanted the changes to happen for them, instead of to them. They demanded the BeltLine. The idea was not only accepted, the BeltLine project was owned." Ever since that humbling moment, Ryan understood that this was his contribution to the world. Ryan found his coconut calling, and Atlanta has enjoyed the benefits.

It has been fifteen years since Ryan first unveiled his vision through his thesis paper, and we are just now getting a glimpse of the full vision as we ride our bikes on the beautifully created path. We are seeing the progress, and it has inspired everyone. Ryan will forever be known as the guy behind the BeltLine.

MAKING THINGS BETTER

Progress is simply the daily decision of making things better in a broken world. Gradual betterment. Humans can't fix everything, but we can fix some things. Everyone can do something. Every day we have the opportunity to make decisions that lead us closer to what we are designed to do and be. We are not always in control, but we still have choices. To wisely choose where we are headed is a sign of a decision maker.

Progress, modernization, and sin have caused many of the problems we are called to fix, but progress is also how we will restore that brokenness. We must take one step forward toward betterment. What moves you? What is at the core of that coconut in your life? Make decisions that match this. It will take time, but the daily choices add up to a purposeful collection of decisions called life.

Progress moves us forward toward an intentional life of choice. Ryan told me, "My decision-making style has changed throughout the process. I trust my own intuition much more than when I started. I have learned that if I feel like this is the type of community I would desire, there is a good chance others have that same feeling. I trust myself more than when I started. I have gained confidence in my decisions along the way." As you make more and more intentional choices, you will gain both perspective and confidence.

You will make some choices that aren't right. Know that from the start and know that you still have a choice to make in the aftermath. Reframe the direction and proceed again. C. S. Lewis said, "Progress means getting nearer to the place where you want to be. And if you have taken a wrong turning, then to go forward does not get you any nearer. If you are on the wrong road, progress means doing an about-turn and walking back to the right road; and in that case the man who turns back soonest is the most progressive man."[3] Change course. Advance toward the good. Keep making that choice. Continue to evaluate where you have come to, what you have learned, and how you want to move forward. Progress. Take the next step toward where you ought to be going.

Becoming a decision maker is not for everyone. But if you don't want to curate your life, then others will do it for you. If you want to assume the role of influencing others, you must be a decision maker. If you want to contribute something significant in a broken world, choose to be a decision maker.

So what do you do when you don't know what to do? You will never be able to predict the future. Hopefully I have given you a process for decision making, a style guide to understand more about how you make decisions, and a reminder of your personal philosophy that should drive your important choices. Now, if you have processed all this information and you still don't know what to do about the problem at hand, consider these three questions:

1. Can I Minimize My Options?

The directions of how things could play out can become too broad if you give yourself too much time to mull over your problem. Give yourself a deadline for making a decision. Sometimes the myriad of options can become overwhelming as well. Try limiting your options to two. What are the two choices that are most reasonable and you could reasonably choose between? If you minimize the options, you may see more simply and more precisely the correct choice.

2. Can I Minimize Change?

You may find yourself saying, "If I do this, then this will happen." The change may be huge, the impact too great. The decision may be too overwhelming. The scenario could be too extreme, and this will impact your ability to choose. Instead, minimize the scenario by taking one step in that direction without making wholesale changes. This could result in a smaller impact with the ability to gain more clarity.

For example, I have a friend who wants to write a resource to educate churches throughout the nation about the effect of globalization on missions. He is passionate, and he envisions his future coaching and educating the church in the West about missions. What an enormous undertaking! But he is stuck. He has the information and the huge vision, but how does he choose what to do next? As Andre and I sat and talked to him about his next steps, he felt overwhelmed with how the unfolding of this vision would affect him and his family. Should he move overseas to research more? Should he quit his job to pursue this dream? I stopped him before he got too far ahead of himself. "Scott, have you written any chapters yet?" I asked.

We talked through breaking this big vision down into bite-size decisions that didn't have to seem so drastic. Start local, we said. Take your home church through the resource, get feedback, send the manuscript to publishers, and plan a few trips overseas in the next few years.

What is the simplest decision you can make today to move in the right direction without changing more than is needed? When you make a smaller move in the right direction, you may find greater clarity.

3. Can I Get Help?

After going through your process, sometimes talking it through one last time helps. Ask a friend to meet you for lunch or coffee and talk through it one last time. We need each other in these moments of tension and transition to finish the process. If your friend is a good listener, he or she will repeat your observations and evaluations in a way that could help lead to direction. Your friend will hopefully help guide you toward what to do next.

ONE SMALL STEP FOR A MAN, ONE GIANT LEAP FOR MANKIND

My friend Peyton is the co-owner of a company called Roam.[4] Roam is a coworking place where people can pay for access to an office or meeting space whenever they need it. His commitment to excellence is unmatched, and the services Roam provides are accompanied by a deep sense of responsibility. As culture continues to produce more freelancers working from home, Roam has found a way to bring these dreamers together through a unique environment that fits their needs perfectly. Peyton is the CEO of two locations and is taking the next steps toward more, learning along the way and making proactive decisions daily. Peyton meets with many dreamers who tell him their stories or passions, each looking for wisdom, connections, and affirmation. They desire his advice and often ask him to be one of those people at the table to make decisions.

As the dreamers ask for advice, he consistently shares this simple principle of progress:

> Many people have big dreams, but few people can tell you how to get there or even where to get started. It's the shift from simply a vision to the practice of living out the mission. If you want to go to the moon, that's exciting. I want your dream to come to life. It will be a great story, and I want to see that it happens for you. But there are many steps on your way to the moon. What is the first thing you would do if you were planning a trip to the moon? You would go research NASA. If you are going to the moon, you will have to go through NASA. You might want to see what it takes to get into NASA. What are the schooling requirements, training, or qualifications? Check out the application process. Going to the moon sounds like an amazing dream; now, what is the first step on that journey?

We all have big dreams, but we usually have to take small next steps to bring dreams to life. Dreams are full of steps along the way. Progress.

The dream of the BeltLine costs over one billion dollars. If Ryan needed a billion dollars to make the dream of the Atlanta BeltLine come into existence, he probably needed to start by printing out the map, highlighting where this hidden railroad is found in each of the neighborhoods, and sending it to people to see. To cast vision, he needed to take the next step. For the dream to come into reality, he needed to write letters to every person who could make the dream come to life.

Every piece of progress begins with making the choice to take the next step forward. Write the letter. Look up the address. Buy the stamp. Stuff the package. Seal the envelope. Mail the letter.

The BeltLine is well on its way. The first phase is creating the twenty-two-mile path all the way around the city. If you visited me in Atlanta and I took you on a bike ride through a portion of the space, you would see hundreds of people on the BeltLine running, riding, laughing, and creating art together. You would see the many communities in Atlanta convening together one step at a time. You would see a glimpse of the dream Dr. Martin Luther King Jr. had for our city played out in a vision that a college student imagined. Now I get to write about the movement.

One beautiful fall day our family decided to get together with some friends and walk on the first portion of the BeltLine. The kids rode their bikes and the adults walked along the path with them. The sky was clear with a cool breeze. We stopped at a Mexican restaurant just off the path. Throughout dinner our conversation revolved around how much we loved the BeltLine and were dreaming of the day when it would be totally done and we could ride around the entire loop.

Then all of a sudden we heard it. Thunder. Thunder again, and it was loud. The restaurant had a metal roof and the intense storm deafened our conversation. It began pouring, and our car was about a mile away. So I did what any dad would do in that moment: I looked up the weather on my phone and pulled up the radar map of the storm. It was one of those storms that would not end for about twelve hours.

I remember looking around the table and thinking, *One person has to go get the car: me.* I also made eye contact with the other dad at the table, and though we didn't say a thing, we had a long conversation about what we were about to experience together. In short, we were about to get drenched. He didn't even have a car; he only had bikes, and his bikes could not fit in my car. He needed to ride a bike a mile home, get a car, and come back and pick up the rest of the family.

In the middle of that meeting of the minds, my fifteen-month-old boy, Neko, started getting restless. He was done sitting in the restaurant and was ready to move. Our wonderful Sunday stroll on the BeltLine was turning into a disaster quickly. Somebody had to do something. I turned to Andre and said, "I'm going to get the car." Her face lit up, which I read as some combination of "Thank goodness," "It's about time you said that," "Honey, you are sweet," and "There is no way in the world I am going to get the car." Then I said, "And I'm taking Neko with me."

The words poured out of my mouth before I really had thought it through, but I had a feeling Neko would love it. A moment of adventure for daddy and son to bond in a way we had never done. It was time for action. I picked him up and lifted him onto my shoulders, held his legs close, and started for the door. The other dad got up in the same moment and swiftly snatched his bike. The three of us paused in the frame of the front door of the Mexican restaurant together looking out. The door was open, the rain pouring, and the only way to get this done was to take the next step. Make the decision. Let's go.

I started at a slow jog. As I passed numerous tables of people under awnings, I could feel their judgment. Look at that bad father carrying his little boy in that awful rain. I decided I didn't care; we were doing this, together. I was running on the concrete BeltLine path with Neko bouncing up and down on my shoulders. I was doing what needed to be done and doing it with my son. The decision had been made, and we would not turn back. He was breathing as hard as I was, but something in his body language made me think it was less fear and more fun for him.

Then I heard a chuckle and then a giggle. Soon he started laughing, uncontrollable belly laughing. Laughing out loud as only a kid with no inhibitions could do. He thought running in the downpour was the best thing ever. He was all in. As other people stuck in similar situations frantically passed us, they looked at Neko and started smiling. Though I couldn't see Neko, I got a glimpse of him through their comments: "That kid is awesome." "He is having the time of his life." "I have never seen a smile so amazing." He was like this little beam of sunlight radiating through the dark storm clouds of rain.

As I kept running and running, hearing and feeling my son's laughter and watching the effect he was having on others, I could feel my smile get bigger and bigger. The moment I stepped out of that taco bar started my son and me on an adventure that I would never forget.

When we finally made it to the car and I could take him off my shoulders to look at him, he was blue with cold. But he couldn't stop smiling between shivers. I turned on the heat in the car and quickly stripped him down. Thankfully, we had a dry diaper. When I found one of Andre's sweatshirts to wrap him in, we both started laughing again. Pure joy.

To date, that was the best moment I have had with Neko. I took a step forward and something amazing happened that I never would have planned for or imagined. Ryan Gravel took a step forward with the BeltLine fifteen years ago, and now I was able to experience this moment with my son. We can never be certain of what the future will bring, but daily we get the opportunity to say yes or no.

My favorite television show ever created is *The West Wing*, written by Aaron Sorkin. It's filled with dramatic dialogue that depicts the lives of staffers in the White House. When the show was first released, I was very young and had no interest in watching it; but last year Andre and I decided to see if all the accolades were correct. This was going to take serious commitment: seven seasons, twenty-two to twenty-three episodes per season. That's over six thousand minutes of written dialogue. Unsure of how long we would last, we began.

We were hooked in the first episode. We watched the entire series in less than four months. It is brilliantly written, often including the hardest decision-making moments you could ever imagine.

It made us want to be decision makers. The writing causes you to place yourself in the middle of the White House, imagining yourself as the president of the United States, contemplating decisions that impact an entire nation. It made our current moments of tension seem so elementary in scale, while inspiring us that even in the most complicated of all situations, we have the ability to find solutions. I loved the moments when a conflict was resolved and one of the characters always asked the trademark question: What's next?

Decisions don't end; we just move toward the next one. For the rest of your life you will be put in moments of tension and considering times of transition. As you learn to make good choices, more will come. An intentional collection of choices will be what you are known for. When we choose daily to make something better in a broken world, we experience progress. Progress will allow us to see more and more beauty in a broken world. We will never make progress unless we start using the words *yes* and *no*. The two most powerful words in the dictionary always give the opportunity to bring us closer to our unique design. These choices shape our lives and the lives of others.

Welcome to the life of a decision maker. Yes or no?

TAKE ACTION

What is one decision you are facing that could benefit from the six-step process I've outlined throughout this book? (See near the end of chapter 6 for the list of six steps.) Which steps have you already taken? Which ones have you skipped? Make a plan for walking through the process and getting to a decision point.

QUESTIONS FOR GROUPS

1. What are the most important things you have learned about decision making from this book?
2. When you have a big decision to make, how hard is it for you to reach
   a place of closure, make the decision, and step forward? If that's hard
   for you, what do you think makes you not want to decide?
3. Talk about how each of the following strategies could help you
   move forward: Reducing your options to two. Taking a step forward that involves only a small amount of change. Consulting
   with someone one last time. Which of these strategies strikes you
   as most helpful to you?

NOTES

Chapter 1: This or That

1. Willard F. Harley Jr., *His Needs, Her Needs: Building an Affair-Proof Marriage* (Grand Rapids, MI: Fleming H. Revell, 2001), 208.

2. Malcolm Gladwell, *Blink: The Power of Thinking without Thinking* (New York: Little, Brown, 2005).

3. Brad Lomenick, *The Catalyst Leader: 8 Essentials for Becoming a Change Maker* (Nashville: Nelson, 2013).

4. Donald Miller, "An Incredible Reminder of How Short Life Really Is," *Storyline* (blog), http://storylineblog.com/2013/04/09/an-incredible-reminder-of-how-short-life-really-is/.

5. John S. Hammond, Ralph L. Keeney, and Howard Raiffa, *Smart Choices: A Practical Guide to Making Better Decisions* (Boston: Harvard Business School, 1999), 1–4.

Chapter 2: My Story

1. Stephen R. Covey, *The 7 Habits of Highly Effective People: Powerful Lessons in Personal Change* (New York: Simon & Schuster), 115.

2. "'Content Is King, but Platform Is Queen': PW Talks with Michael Hyatt," by Natalie Danford, *Publishers Weekly*, May 18, 2012, www.publishersweekly.com/pw/by-topic/authors/interviews /article/52017-content-is-king-but-platform-is-queen-pw-talks -with-michael-hyatt.html.

3. Learn more about Q at www.qideas.org.

4. John C. Maxwell, *The Power of Leadership* (Colorado Springs: Honor Books, 2001), 94.

5. To learn more about Eddie Kirkland, go to www.eddiekirkland writes.com.

6. To learn more about the Parish, go to parishanglican.org.

7. Henry Cloud and John Townsend, *Boundaries: When to Say Yes, How to Say No to Take Control of Your Life* (Grand Rapids, MI: Zondervan, 1992), 31.

8. Cloud and Townsend, *Boundaries*, 200.

Chapter 3: I Heart

1. You can see the video at kidpresident.com.

2. Eric Barker, "8 Things the World's Most Successful People All Have in Common," *Time*, March 5, 2014, http://time. com/12670/8-things-the-worlds-most-successful-people-all-have -in-common/?utm_content=buffer968b8&utm_medium =social&utm_source=twitter.com&utm_campaign=buffer.

3. For more on Esther, see www.estherhavens.com.

4. C. S. Lewis, *The Four Loves* (Orlando: Harcourt Books, 1988), 121.

5. Brené Brown, *Daring Greatly: How the Courage to Be Vulnerable Transforms the Way We Live, Love, Parent and Lead* (New York: Gotham Books, 2012), iBook ebook, 500–501.

6. Brown, *Daring Greatly.*

Chapter 4: Life Curated

1. This phrase was coined by Klayton Korver and Seer Outfitters.
2. "About Us," Bearings, accessed May 14, 2014, www.bearingsguide .com/about/.
3. "Curators vs. Consumers," Bearings, accessed May 14, 2014, www.bearingsguide.com/2011/04/18/curators-vs-consumers/.

Chapter 5: Problem Solvers

1. For more on this organization, see www.wordmadeflesh.org.

Chapter 6: Decision-Making Styles

1. See littlemissmatched.com.
2. Erica Goode, "How Culture Molds Habits of Thoughts," *New York Times*, August 8, 2000.

Chapter 7: A Pile of Chips

1. Chip Heath and Dan Heath, *Decisive: How to Make Better Choices in Life and Work* (New York: Crown Business, 2013), 87.
2. Keith Yamashita and Sandra Spataro, *Unstuck: A Tool for Yourself, Your Team, and Your World* (New York: Portfolio, 2004), 153.
3. Ken Robinson, *Out of Our Minds: Learning to Be Creative*, rev. ed. (Chichester, UK: Capstone, 2011), 220.
4. Inspired by a practice called the Options Test in Heath and Heath, *Decisive*, 87.

Chapter 8: People Matter

1. Scott Belsky, *Making Ideas Happen: Overcoming the Obstacles Between Vision and Reality* (New York: Portfolio, 2010), 44.

Chapter 9: Welcome to the Table

1. For more on Clay's woodworking, see www.rustictrades.com.
2. See www.movinginthespirit.org.

Chapter 10: Swimming to the Sandbar

1. Tom Rath, *StrengthsFinder 2.0* (New York: Gallup, 2007), 9.
2. Elizabeth Gilbert, *Committed: A Skeptic Makes Peace with Marriage* (New York: Viking, 2010), 45.
3. Erwin Raphael McManus, *The Artisan Soul: Crafting Your Life into a Work of Art* (San Francisco: HarperOne, 2014), 7.
4. Charles T. Lee, *Good Idea. Now What?: How to Move Ideas to Execution* (New York: Wiley, 2012), 49.
5. See xkmacarons.com.
6. Gregory Boyle, *Tattoos on the Heart: The Power of Boundless Compassion* (New York: Free Press, 2010), 121.
7. Tom Paterson, *Living the Life You Were Meant to Live* (Nashville: Nelson, 1998), 21.
8. Jia Jiang, "100 Days of Rejection Therapy," *Fearbuster* (blog), www.fearbuster.com/100-days-of-rejection-therapy/.
9. See www.fearbuster.com/2012/11/18/day-3-rejection-therapy-ask -for-olympic-symbol-doughnuts-jackie-delivers/.
10. For more information, see urbanperform.org.

Chapter 11: The Quiet in the Storm

1. Inspired by Henri J. M. Nouwen, *Out of Solitude: Three Meditations on the Christian Life* (Notre Dame, IN: Ave Maria, 1974), 22.
2. Susan M. Heathfield, "Creative Thinking Matters: Bill Gates Looked for Creative Thinking," About.com, Human Resources, accessed April 5, 2014, http://humanresources.about.com/od/motivationsucces3/a/learn_read.htm.
3. This question was taught to me by Michael Metzger through *The Society Room Lectures*.
4. Andy Stanley, *The Best Question Ever: A Revolutionary Approach to Decision Making* (Colorado Springs: Multnomah, 2004), 169.

Chapter 12: A Run on the BeltLine

1. "The Atlanta BeltLine: The 5 *Ws* and Then Some," Atlanta Beltline, accessed May 17, 2014, http://beltline.org/about/the-atlanta-beltline-project/atlanta-beltline-overview/.
2. "Le Viaduc des Arts," Le Viaduc des Arts, accessed April 5, 2014, www.leviaducdesarts.com.
3. C. S. Lewis, *Mere Christianity* (New York: HarperOne, 2000), 28.
4. See meetatroam.com.

BE A PROBLEM SOLVER

JOIN AN INNOVATIVE COMMUNITY
ADDRESSING SOCIAL NEEDS

PLYWOOD

WWW.PLYWOODPEOPLE.COM

WHAT IS ENOUGH?

This book is about generosity.
We have been given much, and need to wrestle with what our responsibility is with what we have been given.

[+] [-]

"How much is enough? In this important and engaging new book, Jeff makes it clear that when it comes to generosity, connection, and community, too much isn't enough."

SETH GODIN, author of *The Icarus Deception*

David C Cook
transforming lives together